To my wonderful
neighbor Janet.
May God bless you as you read
what God gave me to write.

Jerry Thomas

But You

D1478581

**"O MAN OF GOD,
FLEE THESE THINGS,
AND PURSUE RIGHTEOUSNESS"**
Paul the Apostle wrote to Timothy,
his true son in the faith

Part One, The Journal
Part Two, To The Beginning
Part Three, And Beyond

A novel by
Jerry Thomas

But You - Copyright © 2022 All rights reserved.

Cover design - Jerry Thomas
Illustrations - Jerry Thomas

No part of this publication may be reproduced, distributed, or transmitted in any form or by any means, including photocopying, recording, or other electronic or mechanical methods, without the prior written permission of the copyright owner, except in the case of brief quotations embodied in critical reviews and certain other noncommercial uses permitted by copyright law.

Some of this book is a work of fiction. In this publication any names, descriptions, entities, and incidents, other than Scripture references, are products of the author's imagination. If there is any resemblance to actual persons, events, and entities, it is entirely coincidental.

Published by BookBaby

Scripture taken from the New King James Version ®. Copyright © 1982 by Thomas Nelson. Used by permission. All rights reserved.

Print ISBN: 978-1-66785-734-3
eBook ISBN: 978-1-66785-735-0

Printed in the United States of America on SFI Certified paper.

First Edition

More thanks than I have room here to express...

First and foremost is my gratitude to the Lord our God for His perfect love and guidance through every chapter in this book.

Marilyn, my wife, for spending endless hours helping to edit this work. But more than anything, for her neverending encouragement, prayers, and faith in me to finish. She has been an inspiration to me from the start.

Doris Smith, an accomplished author herself, for her encouragement and advice that was an immeasurable asset for me. Her and her husband's friendship have meant so much.

Pastor Lance Stiver, whose wonderful Spirit-filled sermons were instrumental in guiding me through several chapters. When I was "stuck" on one issue or another, his sermon that next Sunday was often the answer that I needed.

Pastor Jim Halstead, for his lifelong evangelical mindset that has always been an inspiration for me to reach out more and more to the lost.

Pastor Brian Scott...Thanks for your apostolic teaching, and just as much thanks for your friendship. I miss those times.

Pastor Lee Miller and his wife Martha. Pastor Lee is gone now, but thanks to them for their patient years of mentoring me.

Many other names I could mention, certainly. Men and women who have become fellow disciples in Christ. Thanks to all of you for your love and friendship.

I made a promise to my fifth grade football and basketball coach that if I ever wrote a book, I would thank him for his Christ-like character while in school. He has always shown us boys what being a Christ-centered leader was supposed to look like.Thank you Mr. Retig

Contents

PART ONE
The Journal

But You

The Journal

1

Discovery

A forgiven minister of God's Word

Prior to being introduced to Pastor Jimmy Lee Cambridge, Mark Garner believed that there was a God who created everything. He also believed in Jesus, because he had attended parochial school for six of his first eight years of education. However, he was not positive about most everything else. Although he had been taught from the catechism and the Bible in those early years, it didn't seem to take. His seventh and eighth grade years were in public school. He and his sister had grown up in a very dysfunctional home, and he was not the best of students, but he did believe in God. As it happened though, one night many years later while complaining about his life condition, God miraculously drew Mark's heart to Him. Then, through a series of events, He led him to a rather large store front church, way across town. That first Sunday Mark attended church there, he came face to face with this six-foot six-inch man who presented himself as a kind, patient, caring teacher of God's Word. Mark did confess later though, that he felt a small charge of intimidation because the pastor was so large. Mark, up until meeting him, was always the one who was in charge, and he could instantly see that he was not going to get away with that here. Looking back, he confessed that since God knew exactly what he needed, Mark was given this much-larger-than-he-was man for him to learn how to submit. Not only to the pastor's teachings, but also to God. Actually, it took Mark years before he was totally convinced of his own inferior thoughts compared to God's holy, perfect, and like it or not, understand it or not, ways. Mark Garner did finally learn how to submit, and how important it was to submit to God and His ways, not to mention what the benefit that total submission to God would bring. Mark will say to you today, "Thanks be to God for all He has done for me!" But he will also say with no reservation, "Thanks to that six-foot, six-inch man of God that He placed in my path. It was because of him that my life was turned around so that I was able to become a true disciple of Jesus."

Mark's first meeting with Pastor Cambridge was almost twenty-five years ago. In time they became each other's prayer and accountability partners, before Mark's dear mentor said goodbye to this world and went on to be with the Lord. But Pastor Jimmy Lee Cambridge will forever be in Mark's heart and mind. He has, and will testify often of how God used Pastor Cambridge to bring his life from a sinning, not knowing or caring man, to a forgiven minister of God's Word. Thus, enabling Mark to help others just like himself find and seek the ways of Christ.

Mark was just about fifteen years younger than Pastor Cambridge when they first met. Mark's life, up to that point, did not show off a smarter than the average bear kind of guy. But in truth he was a very bright man, and certainly smart enough to know the difference between most of the rights and any wrongs that this world seems to ignore, although few ever saw much of that in Mark. He simply chose to look like he had an inferior intellect to get away with his rebellious desires. But he had had enough, and he was thirty-two years old when he gave up his riotous life he had been living to totally embrace this opposite life style. It has been said that the percentage of persons who are willing to totally accept the true Christian walk after the age of thirty decreases exponentially, but Mark was one who defied the odds.

Pastor Cambridge was in his mid-forties when they met, and his whole life and his entire ministry was wrapped around the one Scripture Jesus told His disciples to basically "teach them to obey all that I have taught you." His sermons could come from anywhere in the Bible, but almost always ended with how to apply that last command that Jesus gave his disciples when he ascended into heaven. He had completed seminary in nineteen seventy-nine, and spent the next several years as assistant pastor of a church in New York. Then the denomination helped him and his wife Martha open a brand-new church here at home. That had been over a dozen years prior to Mark walking in shy and disheartened with the way his life had turned out thus far. Mark wasn't looking for a church exactly, he was just roaming the area on foot and came across it. From that first Sunday morning though, when Pastor Cambridge invited Mark to meet with him one day that week, "I would really like to get to know you," he said, "and how it was that you came to find us here," to the better part of two and a half decades later, the two of them had become best friends and prayer partners.

It only took a couple of sessions of mentoring from Pastor for Mark to be absolutely positive that he was in the right place. It took over two years, however, for Mark to be versed enough to minister God's grace to others semi-successfully, and it took an additional year before Mark would be considered absolutely qualified to be a minister of God's Word as lay leader. He had been mentored well, and given opportunity to prove that he knew how to use God's Word by demonstrating what he had learned in a variety of circumstances. He had been shadowed by the pastor until he was able to stand on his own. Mark had not even completed high school up to the time he walked into Pastor Cambridge's church, so those fairly in-depth studies he was given by Pastor that he was completing with excellence surprised everyone, including Mark himself. Sometime during that training though, he was also encouraged to apply for his GED, and he passed that with flying colors as well.

During those twenty plus years of serving God together, literally hundreds of stories can be testified of God's wonderful ways and blessings. Memories that are used even today to bring hope to many. Pastor Jimmy and Mark spent many hours and days walking the streets bringing the good news to many people and to anyone they would meet along the way. And it was through Pastor's leadership that many others also learned to minister outside the church. Some ministered in the jail, some in the rescue mission, the crisis pregnancy center, and anywhere else God would lead. Even to holding evening church services to really low-income members of a broken-down trailer park, where most of them living there had no transportation to be able to come to church on Sunday. So, it came as a pretty great surprise, during one of their last one-on-one weekly prayer and accountability meetings, that his beloved pastor confided in him, "I've been a pastor now for over forty years, and sometimes I can't see much fruit from my efforts. What do you think?" Mark tells the story now that he was totally awestruck when he heard his pastor make that statement.

"What do I think?" Mark said when he was able to speak. "What do I think?" he said again incredulously. And Mark went on to try to spell out all the things he could remember of what this six-foot, six-inch humble man of God had been a part of, ending with a hope that he, Mark, could replicate just some of what Pastor Jimmy Lee Cambridge had accomplished for the kingdom of God.

It was also during that same meeting, Mark recalls, that Pastor told Mark that he was only asking God for seventy years. "What an ominous thing to say," Mark remembers thinking, since he knew that Pastor was already sixty-nine, so he countered with, "What if God gives you seventy-one years? What then will you ask God for?" He remembered that both of them laughed about that then. It was about a month later that Pastor was diagnosed with bone cancer, and that he was in a very serious stage, indicating little chance of survival. He did allow some treatment, but in the end chose to let the illness take its course. It was about a year after that when Mark got the anticipated phone call from Martha of his passing, and don't you know, Pastor Jimmy Lee Cambridge was seventy years and a month old when he said his goodbyes. It brought both sadness and a blessing to Mark at the same time. His funeral told the story of Pastor Jimmy Lee Cambridge's life, and it saddened Mark that his mentor could not be there in person to see and hear the literally hundreds of testimonies of his dedication, his faithfulness, and his humble Christ-like character. Mark stood alone at one point facing his pastor's casket and thinking, "This is the best friend I have ever known." He truly was like a brother to Mark, although early on, he would say that he was more like the father he never had. As the years passed though, brother is what they both ended up with. Silently he shouted from his spirit, "Way to go, Pastor. I'll be seeing you sometime later."

You Have My Complete Attention

About three days after the funeral, Mark received a phone call from Martha, asking him to make some time for the two of them to meet on a very important issue. "Well of course I will," Mark said without hesitation. "What's it all about?"

"I'll show you when we get together," she said, "but I'll need you to give me at least an hour. Would that be, okay?" So, they set an appointment for the following Saturday morning.

"Are you doing alright?" Mark questioned when she opened the door. "When you called you sounded so serious. Is there something you need me to help you with?"

"No, I'm fine," she said very softly, and assuredly. "No, it's something that I'm going to help you with. You know how close Jimmy was to you. He loved you as a brother more than you could possibly know. Come sit down, have some coffee, and I'll tell you a story."

"This still sounds serious, Martha, really serious," Mark said as he pulled out a chair. "I have to wonder is something wrong, because this is so soon after Pastor's funeral."

"I'm fine, I told you." Martha assured him. "This is something we talked about doing when we first found out he was terminal. Just relax. You'll understand as we get started." She turned, walked to the counter behind them and poured two cups of coffee. She set one in front of Mark, and then sat down in a chair across from him. "First of all, the reason he wanted me to wait until after he was gone to meet with you was because he wasn't sure obviously when, exactly, he was going to die. And also, he felt he might have more to write," and with that she pulled a very old looking, tattered three-ring binder from a huge canvas tote, and pushed it across the table at Mark. "This is one of four notebooks that Jimmy has journaled in for about forty years, and they are now yours."

"What's," was all Mark got out when Martha cut him off.

"That, Mark, is one of the journals Jimmy has been ledgering in from the very first church service we had in our new church. He had been journaling since his first year in seminary, but he asked that I remove those years. He didn't even tell me about his journaling for over a year. He wasn't keeping it a secret from me, he said, but just wanted to keep track of his studies and what he felt he was learning from each Sunday church service we attended. He told me that it would help him when he had to start his own church."

"Did it help him? And, wow, look at all these entries." Mark began to page slowly through that first binder. "And you say that he had four of these?"

"As it turned out, he ended up with one new binder for each ten years. That first one there, you'll notice is from 1984 to 1994. The other ones are the same with each covering a ten-year span."

Mark turned some of the pages reverently, because they were so old and weathered. Some he noticed were slightly torn. Others had extra markings, like he was referencing something else.

"And," Martha said, "in answer to your first question, it did help, certainly, but more than that it started Jimmy down a path that you know was his real calling for the ministry. He was the pastor and shepherd of our church, and he performed that excellently, as you know. But Jimmy's real calling was more in the line of mentoring men who believed in the Creator of the universe without reservation, but who needed training on how to use God's Word for His glory. He always kept an eye out for that one person who had an endless desire to learn. That would be you, Mark. He saw that spark in you from the first day you walked into our store front church we started over there on the bypass. You had that 'I really want to know' look on your face. We both saw it. He watched you grow into a minister of God's Word. More than any other man he has been privileged to mentor, Mark, you were the one right from the start who he always said was one who would never turn back. At one time he entertained the thought of sending you to seminary to become a pastor in your own right."

Mark stiffened, and momentarily pulled his face up into a comical grimace at that last statement. "That would never have happened."

"Yeah, I know." Martha followed quickly. "That was never God's calling on your life. It was in Jimmy's mind, though, when he started mentoring you. He discovered that it wasn't going to be, when he figured out what kind of ministry God was using you for. He was considering you for Brighten Theological, though, just so you know. We both saw, and of course you know too, what your real calling is. With your evangelical heart and that outreach of yours to the city, Pastor would have had a great deal of difficulty even thinking about finding, let alone reaching anyone in the inner city like you have."

"Wait a minute," Mark said raising his hands in a protest kind of way. "Pastor always wanted to go with me when I started hitting the streets like I did. Unless he had something very important to take care of, he always went."

Martha smiled gently at Mark, and caught and kept his eye for a long time and said nothing at all. She just kindly stared at him.

"What?" Mark finally countered. "What?" he said again.

"Mark, think back to when you two started doing that. Whose idea was it? Which one of you two came up with the demographics? Who was it that spent your vacation from your job to plan your "City Outreach?" Who was it that went to all those other inner-city churches on your days off, to encourage them to join you? Mark, you came up with all that on your own, and that, of course is your calling. Pastor, although he loved all those times he could go with you, still knew that it was you, not him, who God was using for that particular outreach. And that is why he wanted you to have this journal of his."

"Okay Martha, you have my complete attention. Oh, and I hope you know how much I loved Pastor as if he was my brother as well."

"Yes, I do know, but more importantly, so did Jimmy. Here's what he is asking you to do. Don't be too quick to finish reading through all of those notebooks he journaled in, but don't dawdle either. What he was looking to accomplish was for you to pray over all the pages before you read, and then read it with that 'I just want to see what you want me to see, Lord,' gifting of yours."

We know," Martha continued, "that it will surely be a challenge for you. We don't know how many pages there are in each of his four binders, but we guessed at about two hundred and fifty. He came up with that number because of how he would journal. He had one page for each month. At the top of that page, he would record the month and year, and then under that he would write the day and date of his entry. So, he would have four or five lines for each Sunday of the month, and he only journaled on Sundays after church. That would make twelve pages a year, roughly, and of course that would equal one hundred and twenty pages for each notebook for the ten years. Now he often had extra things he wanted to journal about, so he would place a circle around any Sunday date where he wanted to include additional information, pull out a separate page, make his notes, date it, and place it behind that month's recordings. Sometimes he would have an extra sheet or even two for one Sunday, or maybe one page for each of a couple of Sundays. Anyway, he estimated that he may have an additional dozen or so pages per year that way, so he ended up with what he figured was an average twenty-five or so pages a year, and of course that gave us the 250 pages per decade, give or take a dozen pages or so. It doesn't matter anyway, but we both wanted you to know what you were being asked to dive into. As the years went by, his notes increased in size some - but he figured on the average, and he came up with that number. The first entry is titled Christmas Eve service, nineteen eighty-four. His last entry, was about a month ago."

Mark," and Martha paused briefly before going on, "you know that he hasn't been in the pulpit for many months now, well, I guess it's almost a year, so his last entries are quite revealing. It wasn't until then that he even thought of giving this to anyone to read. Until then it was just his personal journaling that carried no particular design for anyone, for any reason. But then, one morning, oh let's see, maybe six weeks ago, or it could have been a couple of months now, he told me what he wanted to do with it, and here we are. I am thankful that District has provided some really great interim pastors, because that has given us time to put this all together for you. He wanted you to enjoy his writings certainly, for the gift that it is, but most importantly he is giving you an assignment."

"What assignment is he giving me? What am I supposed to be looking for?" Mark asked.

"Jimmy told me that he would not give you an answer for that question, and he knew you were going to ask. He just said that God will show it to you, or not. 'Just give him my journals,' Jimmy said, 'and tell him to be diligent and pay very close attention to all of my notes.' I guess that is the assignment."

Mark lowered his head to this seemingly giant, but wonderful task. Again, he began to thumb slowly through some of the pages of this now almost forty-year-old notebook. He made low indistinguishable sounds every once in a while, that one might interpret as different forms of WOW. After a few minutes he closed the notebook, and looked up to his benefactor. "Martha," he said, "this is such a beautiful gift. Thank you so much. Could I have the tote there as well?"

"Sure, you can. It may be the best way for you to carry these four journals of his. I was going to give it to you anyway. Now, you take as long as you like on this, ah, well," she hesitated, "but don't dawdle, like I said. Just read it at your own pace. I think Jimmy knew your heart for study, and we both expect you to enjoy it as much as what you will learn from it. I would ask, though, if you don't mind, to keep me in the loop. I would greatly appreciate that." They finished their coffee with memories that produced some tears, and some laughter. Mark said that he was excited, and couldn't wait to get started, and with that Martha stood and walked Mark to the door. "I'll see you in church on Sunday," she said.

Mark just raised his free hand to her over the back of his head as he departed, "Thanks, and bye."

_____
_____

But You
The Journal

2

Investigation

Discover, Or Not

A few days passed before Mark was able to sit down to open the first of his pastor's four journals. He had pulled it out of the case and placed it on his desk right after he got home on Saturday, but wasn't quite ready to dive into it. He wanted to make sure that he had cleared his entire agenda, so that nothing would get in his way. Mark was one of those people who once he started something, literally, HAD to finish it. He always lived with the ideal Pastor Cambridge taught him. "Do it right, or don't do it at all." Mark approached everything with that front-end ideal that he had to finish well. So, for those first few days, he just analyzed his beloved pastor's forty years of journaling. Briefly, as he walked by it while on mission for another task he had to finish, he just glanced over at it sitting on his desk. He would stop in awe for a moment and ponder on what it was that Pastor wanted him to find in his journal that took him decades to write. Every night after work he would mull over this task that was issued to him. He just wanted to be a good steward of this precious item gifted to him. It was on that next Thursday evening that he finally sat down and began to pray and then read. "Right next to you again, Pastor," he said to himself, "I'm here to hear from you, as always." And then he prayed, "please open Your truths to me, Lord."

December 1984

Monday the 24th. Christmas Eve; As usual, Christmas Eve service was decently well attended. Message, of course, was the birth of Jesus.   Mary and Joseph, and the ride into Bethlehem, and Jesus. The shepherds, the angels, and the wise men. I did receive some discussion from Alvarez after the service, for introducing the point that "you need to know for sure 'why' Jesus came, in order to know for sure 'if' he came at all. Need to pray for Alvarez.

"Okay," Mark thought. "I don't see anything that would bring concern to Pastor there. "Well," he reconsidered. "Unless it was for this Alvarez." Mark never knew him. He had come and gone before Mark's time. Mark had glanced, inadvertently, at the clock when he started reading that first note, and when he had finished reading through July of eighty-five, he had been reading for about an hour and a half. It was, in his imagination, like having Pastor Cambridge back again to share with. He looked back and counted twenty-seven entries he had finished. "Did I bust through these too quickly?" he thought. "No," he answered his own question. "No, I'm sure I didn't," he followed after a moment. "I spent a little time after finishing each note," Mark said out loud to encourage himself. "I looked for any lesson to be learned, or some point the pastor wanted to make. No, none that I could see." He noticed that there wasn't an entry for every Sunday. He saw that two were missing for June of that last year. He also took the time to look up any Scripture references that Pastor left occasionally on some of his notes, but he didn't see any additional pages that Pastor added like Martha said he had done.

Mark spent the next couple of weeks to finish eighty-five and all of eighty-six, because he started to find extra pages to read. He would stop and ponder on them. He finally concluded that he was making this harder than it was supposed to be, "or not?" He wasn't sure. He found himself talking to his old pastor as he finished almost every one of Pastor's Sunday journals. "Wow, that was good." Or "I'll bet there was more to that sermon." Or "I wish I could have been there to hear that." Or simply, "I do miss you, Pastor Cambridge." He wanted to keep his promise to Martha by "keeping her in the loop," as she had requested, so he called her one evening to report.

"Hello Mark," came her familiar voice, "how's it going?"

"Doing good. Just called to let you know where I'm at so far."

"You want to come over for some coffee again, maybe this Saturday?"

"I was hoping you would ask. Sure, about ten like before?"

She agreed that ten was workable, and when he showed up, she once again had a pot of coffee on just waiting for him. "I can't wait to hear what you may have found out."

"Well, I have been reading, but the truth is that I haven't learned anything yet that I didn't already know, mostly. I mean, I loved his notes, and you know he wrote the way he talked. I could almost hear him speaking to me from those pages. But I don't think that I have read anything other than his sermon notes and what he thought they meant, or some special prayer request, or, oh, I don't know. I guess I'm not sure what I am supposed to be looking for."

"How far did you get," she asked?

"All the way through eighty-six. I'm just about to read his first entry he made for eighty-seven."

"Okay," she nodded, "you wouldn't have seen anything out of the ordinary up to that time."

"That time?" Mark looked mildly alerted. "That time?" He questioned again. "That sounds like I definitely will at some point, and, it also tells me that you know what it is that I will notice, and at what time, ah year I mean, that I will notice it. Do you have some advance knowledge you could share with me?"

"No, Mark, I won't share anything with you. I, well and Jimmy also, wanted to give you absolutely no information at all. We wanted you to discover, or not, all that may be there to discover."

"So, there is something special I am," and he paused looking at her, "supposed to discover, right? It might help me to know what it is, don't you think?"

"Mark, ask yourself. Don't you think that this is a bit of a strange thing to ask someone to do, if it were just for an interesting joy-ride of an inheritance gift? So, yes, of course there is something special we are hoping you will discover, but it is you who needs to," and she emphasized the word again, "discover, or not, what that something is. Just keep reading."

"This sounds like a test, or a riddle," Mark countered, and then after a long pause continued. "Maybe it's one of those 'aliens really do exist theories.' Or maybe it's all about some hidden treasure, or some secret society conspiracy I'm supposed to uncover?"

"Oh, that's great Mark…can't you see Jimmy locked into anything like that?" and they both had a great laugh.

They both sat in silence for a while, and then Mark peeped up over his glasses at Martha like a child might after getting his hand caught in the cookie jar. "I like riddles, Martha," he said softly, like it was a secret he was sharing with her, "you know that."

"I do," and she smiled at him with understanding.

Mark chuckled lightly, and then said, "It's not that difficult of a task I have been given here, and I was enjoying it, but now it has just turned into an exciting puzzle for me to solve."

Mark fell silent again for a moment. "Well," Mark announced, "I guess I will have more fun than I anticipated. I will be sure to let you know the moment, ah I know anything, if," he mused, "I actually do in fact find anything to know."

"That's fine, Mark," she said, and she reached across the table to pat Mark on the wrist. "Either way, you know you are welcome any time," and with that Mark was off with a simple thanks for the coffee, that he didn't finish, and a wave over the back of his head like he did before. He was more excited now than ever, though, because one of Mark's passions was to solve riddles and puzzles and the like. "The harder the better," he would say, and this one just turned into a whopper.

"Bye," was all Martha could muster in that rapid disappearing act Mark just pulled off.

We Really See Its Consequence Now, Don't We?

Mark went directly home and opened up the 1984-1994 notebook to where he had left off. He began to read with a completely renewed excitement. He got through three Sunday's notes so fast it sounded like he was reading an escape procedure from a sinking ship, and he was on it. Suddenly he stopped mid-mango and realized that he was missing everything. "Okay, Lord," he prayed, "I'll slow down." He prayed for help with what he was reading, and started over. Mark only stopped pouring over his old pastor's writings long enough to go to the bathroom and to get another cup of coffee.

Finally, he gave up the fight, and checked out for a good night's rest.

He had continued nonstop every evening from the time he got home from work and ate his dinner, to as late at night as he felt he could. One night after a couple of hours he halted his progress to stand and stretch his legs. But there was something more. He had a sense of importance to consider about that last entry he encountered. "That's interesting," Mark pondered. "It's important too, but…hmmm, I wonder." He sat back down at his desk to re-read what Pastor had recorded for that Sunday.

June 1989

Sunday the 25th. Twenty-seven years ago, this date, the Supreme Court banned all school sponsored prayer in all public schools across America. Individuals could still pray privately, or in groups on school grounds, as long as they didn't disrupt anyone else. But the link between seeking God's direction, correctness, and His ethics was broken completely between the young minds of our land and their educational leaders. I would love to be able to take a poll of that time to find out how many teachers actually agreed that "that" was a very bad move. My sermon this morning was on praying always for our Supreme Court, our nation's children, especially those who attend public schools.

Mark had to stop and do some math, but finally established that he would still have been walking outside of God's will in June of eighty-nine. He remembered hearing something on the news during that year about the Supreme Court's verdict from nineteen sixty-two, and thinking, "So what, who cares anyway? Let them pray to God on their own time and place if they have to. Why should all the rest of us be forced to go through all that religious stuff?" Mark instantly felt a tight pang in his heart at that memory. He, like so many other Americans, just bought into that separation of church and state, but not necessarily because they agreed with the Supreme Court's decision. The majority of people had no trouble with prayer in public school. Even a high number of Americans, Mark thought, including many non-Christians, felt that it might be wrong to ban public prayer, but in the end simply considered that act to be out of their hands. And those who did actually oppose the decision were outnumbered seemingly thousands to one, if you add the silent majority numbers into the mix. But then, they had no way of turning it around anyway. So, they just lived with it. And with that one entry Pastor had written from nineteen eighty-nine, Mark was finally tuned into what he was supposed to be looking for. He jumped up and called Martha on the spot. It was a little later than he normally would have, but he couldn't wait.

Right when she picked up the phone, "Martha Cambridge," he always used her full name when he had something important to tell her, and this epiphany moment of his certainly applied. "I got it," he continued without even allowing her to speak. "Honestly, I got it," he repeated.

"Okay," she soothed, "slow down and tell me about it."

"June twenty-fifth, nineteen eighty-nine, he wrote that his sermon that Sunday was on praying always for our Supreme Court, our nation's children, especially those who attend public schools. He referenced the Supreme Court's ruling from nineteen sixty-two on that date, when they banned school sponsored prayer in all public schools in America. I remembered where and how I was in June of eighty-nine, and it brought me to my knees, in my heart that is. It was a sign of times to come, wasn't it? And there were so few who really grasped its importance. Right? I mean, I didn't, and I was in my mid-twenties then. We really see its consequence now, don't we?"

"Brace yourself, Mark," Martha said. "We thought that you might be affected this way when you got to that point in his first journal. Let me share what Jimmy didn't record. I wasn't supposed to give you any additional information, until, or if you came up with something like this on your own, and you did. So, after that Sunday service, Jimmy announced that we were setting up a special night of prayer for that and similar issues that we were beginning to face in the world around us. All agreed, so he then asked for a show of hands as to which day of the week would work best for most of the people. We ended up with twenty-eight volunteers to attend that prayer time, from then on, at seven in the evening for one half hour. It was to be a special prayer night dedicated to be praying for our nation's Supreme Court, and for all the school kids in America, but specifically those in public schools. Twenty-eight was a pretty good number, understanding that some worked evenings, and some had pre-scheduled events etc."

"I'll buy that," Mark said, "so what happened?"

"That," Martha said sadly, "is what Pastor has been in study and prayer about ever since."

"Ever since?" Mark threw it back at Martha.

"You see, that first Monday evening, we had more than the twenty-eight show up. In fact, we counted somewhere north of forty. We were all so excited. Forty plus came when only twenty-eight signed up. But on the very next Monday night the number had dropped to only twelve, and then just two weeks later, we saw only three, and it never got any better. Even after constant reminders, we only saw one or two others occasionally show up, but generally it was those three and Jimmy and myself."

"Why?" Mark quizzed. "What happened? Did someone die, or something?"

"No, Mark, no one died. But that was an eye-opener for Jimmy and me. That was the first time since we started our church that we openly asked anyone of our congregation to participate in anything outside our regular Sunday fellowship, or any of our eating-n-greeting meetings. The good news was, though, that those three were as faithful as anyone could ask for, and we continued in prayer that way for a couple of years. But, as always, that too finally faded into a non-attended side note in our church history book. Eventually we believed, and it was confirmed, that the reason for that lacking was because the ruling had been so long ago that nothing could be done about it now, so they just gave up. Jimmy and I never did stop praying for our nation that way."

Mark slumped down in his office chair half studying Pastor's journal still open to that same page, and said, "That was what, thirty some years ago, and it's gotten so much worse since...," and his voice just trailed off. It sounded to Martha like Mark felt discouraged.

"Don't you give up, kiddo," and she always called him "kiddo" when she was attempting to mother him, although he was far too old for her to be his mother. "You keep reading. There is so much more for you to do, and we need you to stay focused. There are still thousands, millions of Christians across our land who are silently looking for answers. You may be one of the ones God will use to broadcast some of those. Remember the motto you yourself brought to all of us every time one of us was in some form of discouragement, and feeling like we wanted to give up. You remember?"

"Oh, I'm not the least bit discouraged, Martha." Mark corrected. "I am a bit miffed, but I am fully aware of what is, and has been going on. And I didn't call just to tell you about this one entry. I called to tell you I understand, or at least I think I understand what I am supposed to be looking for now. This one entry is just a starter, and yeah, I remember that motto of mine," and with that Mark stood up, gripping the phone receiver with a little more power. "You bet I remember. 'Quitters lose', he said, "and that's all there is to that. You're a jewel Martha Cambridge, and I'm not a quitter, and you know that."

"I do know that," Martha said in that famous 'it's all going to be alright' soothing, voice of hers. "And, that is another reason we are trusting you with Jimmy's journals. Talk to you soon."

Mark hung up the phone with a simple, "Bye," and a wave of his hand over the top of his head even though Martha was not there to see him.

Too Strict on What They Called "the Precepts of God"

Mark dove back into the journal and began to read with what he called a new tool in his investigative arsenal. He called it Specific Curiosity. He had a good idea what he was looking for now, and kept that mental tool perpetually sitting on his shoulder for an extra set of eyes skilled at picking up anything that even mildly appeared to need extra attention. He went to bed in the middle of year eighty-nine joyous that he was chosen for this task.

During the next week, he had finished all of eighty-nine, and got all the way through ninety-two. He had just finished the notes Pastor wrote for Christmas Eve, Christmas Day, and New Year's Eve of ninety-two, and had to stop. He was tired, but he looked down at his notes, and saw that he had recorded quite a few different things that he initially thought needed some additional consideration, but in the end decided that there wasn't much to them. He loved reading Pastor's notes on his sermons and his side notes giving additional information and thoughts, but other than what he was now calling "normal," nothing else popped out at him.

Mark was unable to continue for a couple of nights because of other commitments that seemed to just "pop-up", and because he really needed a break. But, on that next Saturday, he got up early, made his breakfast, turned off his phone so as to not be disturbed and opened up Pastor Cambridge's journal to Sunday, January third, nineteen ninety-three. Right from the very first words written there, Mark knew that he once again needed to pray. Those first five words stopped Mark in his tracks and his spirit was instantly alerted. He asked God for discernment, and then continued to read, but with a worried look on his face. This one, he noticed, had two full pages added to his initial note for that Sunday.

January 93

Sunday the 3rd. "Gag me with a spoon?" If I hear that one more time, I will gag someone with a spoon. It started with S.K. She won't stop saying that about everything, and it has become very disruptive to our youth group. The phrase was actually started in the late 70's and early 80's, from the "valley girls" in California, but somehow gained popularity among our youth here, now. That and, "come on, man, it's the nineties." Here's what is so hurtful. I know that she doesn't mean any harm by it, but what she doesn't realize is that it is extremely disrespectful. And don't you know, that I am now hearing it from some of the other kids in the group. It has led to outright rebellion. Sometimes some of them, the leaders in the group, simply refuse to take instruction, or finish the simplest of assignments. They are even asking that we "stop boring them to death from always being forced to study the Bible." Or "can't we just have fun sometimes?" The real harm comes from the parents, who after being asked to curb that attitude in their children, they went on the defensive by addressing several members of the congregation stating the church, and I know that means me, are over restrictive and trying to force their kids into a mold that restricts their creativity. OK....So I finally decided to put an end to it in a meeting last Sunday after church with the parents in question, and basically informed them that it had to stop, and offered an alternative set of phrases that could be used instead. That was received by them, again, as an attempt to put even them in a mold. "What right have you got to do that," was the overall opinion, and they left in a huff. Then during the week, one of the fathers went behind my back, inviting all the elders over to his home without me knowing it, in an attempt to get me fired as head pastor. I found that out from Justin, who is faithful to the church. I know it's God's church, certainly, but I am the one, I believe by biblical standards who is supposed to have the last say-so. I'm not concerned about being in charge, I am concerned about doing the will of God, and about the spiritual wellbeing of our church members, and mostly for the youth. Lord my God, show me what I must do to glorify You in this.

Mark remembered hearing about that incident years later after he started to be mentored by Pastor Cambridge. He recalled Pastor saying that it seemed to work out okay, because the two main families who seemed to want to push the issue left the church. Mark also remembered he was told that just a few months after they left, they joined a very progressive church and that church seemed to take off like a rocket. It grew rapidly with massive membership. Mark looked out of his office window and wondered what in the blazes they were offering over there. And with that memory, Mark took himself back to the time, "What was it, summer of two-thousand? Or maybe the following year when I spent that whole summer visiting other churches seeking volunteers to join us in our City Outreach?" Mark had visited that huge and growing church, and recorded his own personal understandings about what he learned then. He made a mental note for himself to look into that church now, and to re-read his earlier notes, if he could remember where he put them. He also remembered that Pastor Cambridge's entire church body did back him up, including all the elders. Some of the other kids who were affected, or infected, from the three kids who left, understood completely and even confessed that they were just trying to be accepted by the group. There was no more mentioned about that situation, Mark thought, but the last note written for January ninety-three, recorded just four weeks later opened Marks eyes again.

January 93

Sunday the 31st. Last Sunday Greg and Barb, along with Charles and Deborah and their families announced that they were leaving the church effective immediately with some remorse. They said that they loved the church, and the church body, but felt that they needed to find a church that was more in line with their beliefs about God, the Bible, and life in general that fit more comfortably with our modern life styles. Greg could...

Mark stopped reading to mull over that last sentence in his mind. "Needed to find a church that was more in line with 'MY' beliefs about God, the Bible, and life in general??? What?" Mark said out loud. "That fit more comfortably with our modern life styles??? What?" he said again. "What is that? That sounds like we get to choose what, or who God is, and what or how we want God to be like," he angrily exclaimed. "Oh, Pastor, I see why you recorded this!" Mark was silent for a moment, and angry, and noticed that there was a nagging *yeah but* itching at his heart outside the obvious, but he couldn't put his finger on what it might be. It wasn't about this Greg guy either, it was about Pastor Cambridge. "Okay, I'm listening," he said out loud again, but he couldn't get it, so he kept reading.

...not resist ending with, "You know, Pastor, it is the nineties." We prayed for them openly with the church, and wished them well. Today we had a congregational meeting, and I bridged the subject on how we should approach similar situations in the future, and, what looked like the entire congregation backed up our church's stance for any subject to be firmly in line with what the Bible teaches. And on topics where it wasn't directly affirmed in the Bible, the Elder Board would have the last word. *

Mark noticed that there was a small asterisk right after the last word. He looked for where he might find what it referenced, and finally found it clear at the very end of the month of March. "Odd, that." Mark concluded. "Why would he do that? What are you wanting to tell me Pastor?" And not for the last time, Mark was wishing that his old pastor was there to take charge and give him an answer.

March 93

Just a follow up note for January 31st. I have noticed that there is a slight, almost unnoticeable distancing from some of our congregation. Also, I am hearing comments, I know that they didn't know I heard, but things like, "what do you think? Greg and Charles weren't so bad, maybe we should visit their new church. They say it's really growing over there, and that they have wonderful benefits for the kids. Maybe we'll like it.?"

Mark also noticed some additional scribblings on one of his added pages when he got to the end of July that year, and had a little trouble making it out. They didn't seem to fit in with anything else, so he pored over those words Pastor had written there, and noted that his writing looked very erratic. Not like his normal pen that was relatively neat, and seemingly grammatically very correct all the time. Mark got his magnifying glass out and was able to read.

We have been losing members. I don't know what's happening. We hold the same type of services. I even tried to change it up via one of the elders who thought I was getting a little too strict on what he called 'the precepts of God.' "Lighten up," he said, "We're only people," and don't you know he just had to add, "come on Pastor, it's the nineties, you know." Oh, that hurt. We had over eighty members up until last summer, and ever since Bob and his group left, we are seeing a decline in attendance. We see less than fifty attend on any Sunday. Maybe a dozen on

Sunday night, and about the same number on Wednesday night. When I called on some of those who haven't attended recently, a few of them told me that they started going to the same progressive church that Greg and Charles are attending, the one that is growing like a weed, and I know why it's growing like a weed. Their bottom line teach is what I call a "feel good" grasp of the Bible. And it's not only what is being taught from the pulpit that poses an imbalance in the whole truth of God's Word, it's the people who flock there to hear what they want to hear, instead of seeking what God wants them to hear. There's a Scripture that details that exactly in 2 Timothy. Lord help me to stay on path with what you want me to do, and to say, and to teach, regardless of any outcome.

This was extremely disturbing, leaving Mark provoked. His I-can't-believe-this uncontrolled intensity produced a frown that creased his brow, and it would not go away. He could easily see where all this was going now, especially since he had been a part of the church since ninety-seven. He went back to his desk and looked up the Scripture that Pastor Cambridge had referenced. "2 Timothy," he said out loud, "but which chapter and verse?" He found it in chapter 4, verses 3 and 4, and he read it out loud. *"For the time will come when they will not endure sound doctrine but according to their own desires, because they have itching ears, they will heap up for themselves teachers; And they will turn their ears away from the truth and be turned aside to fables."*

"There it is," Mark said. "That's calling a spade a spade, isn't it? That is a serious situation," he went on to say, "that more Christians than we would want to admit are locked into, but how can we get them to see, or should I say, how do we help them to be willing to see?" He dropped the journal down with a light slap against his desk. He pushed his chair back, stood up and began to pace back and forth in deep thought. That *yeah but* bounced back into his thoughts again, and he shifted gears to consider what that was all about. It clearly was concerning Pastor Cambridge. Mark could see how hurt he had been over losing members to "what's the name of that other church?" Mark tried to remember. "Something like Great, or Greater something. Greater Life Center? No, but something like that." Mark also knew, from his writings, that his pastor's hurt wasn't because they chose to go to another church, it was because he was sure that they were not going to be fed all the whole truth from God's Word. But then something changed as Mark marched around his rooms. His condemnation altered slightly from being provoked to being on guard. He sensed that there was something really big at stake to be learned. "And you know what, Pastor," continuing to converse with him, "it has gotten so very much worse since then." Mark had to confess, "I'm frustrated, well, and angry I guess also over these issues now." He was also fearful for so many Christians like he knew Pastor Cambridge must have been, but he was wondering what to do about it, "and that *yeah but* won't leave me alone," Mark thought again. "What is it I am supposed to see here?"

Mark got a cup of coffee, and just sat at his desk for a while in prayer. His thoughts could not be pried from that Greater, whatever its name is church, and how Pastor Cambridge felt about that, but mostly what their teaching might be doing to so many Christians. "But," Mark reminded himself, "it's not just their teachings, is it?" he confessed. "It's all the people, whom I would like to think truly believe that Jesus died for their sins, but WANT," and he patted the top of the journal with his one hand, "to hear what is being taught from their pulpit. They have gone out of their way to belong to that teach because it just feels good to them, or as they have said so often, it just makes sense. They are choosing to not listen to sound doctrine. Instead, they are literally looking for a doctrine that," and Mark went back several pages in the journal to look up exactly what was written. "Here it is," he said, and he read it to himself again, *was more in line with their beliefs about God.* "Wow, don't forget that Mark," he said to himself again, "they want to hear it."

"Okay, Pastor, here it is," Mark concluded doing his best James Cagney. Then, with sincerity, he said, "You've taught me all things clear up until a few months prior to you trading in your consciousness here for a permanent perfect understanding there. You have given me all that I know about the Bible, and what my walk with the Lord is supposed to look like. How to guard my thoughts and my ways trusting in God's Holy Spirit, and," Mark once again was brought to a halt in his thinking because he had to confess again, "I still have a long way to go, don't I? Here I am stewing over that other church." Then Mark smiled as he sat back into his desk chair and mouthed a silent prayer, and after a short pause, he said. "I don't have him here, to give me the answers, do I?" That's where his smile came from. He didn't know how many times he caught himself making that comment.

Mark finished his coffee, and pulled himself up to the desk, and suddenly, "I got it. That's the *yeah but* I can't seem to shake. It's all about how Pastor Cambridge overcame that disappointment and hurt." He pulled his Bible out, and read the verse out loud again. *"But you be watchful in all things, endure afflictions, do the work of an evangelist, fulfill your ministry."* Right there next to verse 4. Well, of course I know that, but that is one hard nut to crack, if you dwell on all that other stuff" he said sarcastically, "and I am, aren't I? Yeah, you are Mark," he said out loud again to himself. Silently he was glad he was all alone. "But you too were frustrated, and even angry, like I am now, weren't you?" Mark continued to talk to his old pastor, "I can read it in your notes. But in the end, you simply did what you always taught me to do all those years. God took your anger and frustration from you, or should I say you gave it to God, when you just concentrated on the task at hand that He gave you to do, didn't you? I understand how it was that you were able to go on with that wonderful mature teaching attitude of yours, in spite of," and he stopped again to think, "that Greater Progressive whatever-its-name-is church. A church that was leading Christians off to follow the more human side of God's promises, instead of the more spiritual side of our Savior, and the truth of what is clearly spelled out in the Bible." He leaned back in his chair and again, "It's my turn now, isn't it?" With that statement, Mark turned one of the more significant pages of his life, although he didn't instantly recognize it. "Okay," he said and it was a prayer, "I want to do that now, so what is my task at hand that YOU want me to concentrate on and what steps do you want me to take? Hmmm, steps," Mark stopped dead in his tracks, lifting his head to peer out of his office window again. "What's that about? Steps," he thought. "I wonder," and he pulled out his own notebook and scribbled some thoughts down to be looked at later.

Mark needed a break, so he grabbed his jacket and keys and decided to take a walk. He ended up a dozen blocks or more down town at a small café he frequented, and sat with a cup of coffee just to think and to clear his head.

He was into his second cup when he found himself being unable to stop thinking about how people are so taken away from easily understood teachings that Jesus gave to us all. "It's right there, plain as day," Mark said just above a whisper. "But then, that would be easier to grasp. How is it that graduated, highly learned men and women of the Bible are led off to a feel-good type of faith?" and Mark was right back into that frustration. He mildly laughed at himself remembering that he was just given the answer on how to overcome that frustration. "But, what do I do about the situation? There doesn't seem to be anything I can do to alter any church's teachings, let alone that one progressive church." Mark was right back there again in his thoughts about, "Well let me give that church a name. I'll just call it 'that other church'." Mark fell silent and still, like he was quietly listening, and then, "Interesting." he said, "Is that the task you want me to concentrate on now? Is there something there that you want me to follow through with? I can't seem to stop thinking about it. What is there about *that other church* that I can't seem to let go of?" he silently mouthed. He did know some things about that church, and sitting here thinking about it now, he remembers some of the things he had learned years ago when he approached them to participate in his city outreach. He remembered that they didn't want to partner with Mark's church, they wanted to control it. When asked why, their representative explained that they didn't agree with our stance on all the "hard core edicts," they called them, "of God the way we did." There was a lot more discussed about their doctrine, our doctrine, etc., but Mark couldn't remember any specifics. Mark did remember that the man he had talked to back then tried, "To get me to leave my church and come over to his church. Like that was going to happen!" Mark said to himself. Mark couldn't remember all of what they talked about back then, but he did remember writing some detailed notes later about that visit and with that, Mark got up, paid his bill, and started his long walk home to look for those notes he had made so many years ago. "And it is interesting," Mark said again, "I'm really not angry anymore at anything, I just need to find out what you want me to know about all this, Lord, before I go on with the journal."

With that, Mark got up, paid his bill for the coffee, and mentally looked forward to his hike home. "Show me, Lord," he said to himself as he walked toward the door.

_____

_____

But You

The Journal

3

That Other Church

The Battle Belongs to the Lord

Mark's long walk home afforded him a special time to think. It wasn't difficult for him, under any conditions, to think deeper about anything than most anyone he knew. But he had discovered that when he took long walks, he could really wrap his seriously in-depth thought machine around any topic he was wondering about.

Mark had never married, and had no children, and he was now in his late fifties. He knew why he had never looked for a wife, but now on his way home, he was mulling over why he had never asked God what He wanted for him. Either way he was a confirmed bachelor. Pastor Cambridge and Martha, "Oh Martha, yeah, her especially," he chuckled, wanted him to find a wife. "Why is that, Lord," he asked, "do women just have to make it happen for some guy who isn't married, to get married? Sneaky matchmakers," Mark said in jest again, "every one of them. Guess that's the way you made them, Lord. Not me, though, they will certainly not catch me." But his smile faded for the truths of why he would never be a married man. His family growing up was enough to scare off any possibility of wanting to have one of his own. He shook his head in an attempt to change the subject he was thinking about. There he was again, caught in his own mental devices delving deeper than he really wanted to go on that topic. "So," he said out loud again, "and listen to me Lord. I do talk to myself." And he unconsciously muscled up a smile at the thought. "You know," he said, "there are only two kinds of us in this world. Those of us who talk to ourselves, and liars," and he chuckled again at that old adage he used so often. "Okay, back to the point. What about that other church? What about them, or it, or whoever?" and he spent the rest of his time walking home trying to remember, "Where did I put those notes?"

When he walked into his house and took off his jacket, he immediately went to his filing cabinet. As soon as he opened the first drawer that he thought might contain a file he was looking for, he just froze. He wasn't surprised at all, just overwhelmed. He knew before he started what he was going to face, but facing it was yet another plane on which to walk. He had never been good at keeping files. And that would be an understatement. But here he was, looking down into a mountain of "Where do I go from here?" He pulled out a huge file labeled *"City Outreach, July 1999."* He knew that although it appeared like a pretty good place to start, he also recognized how totally inept he was at keeping records. He sat down with the file and started to page through the folder one page at a time. He found pages with different suggestions on what to do next. Pages of notes for meetings he attended to help him become better equipped to dive into a ministry for the inner city. Other notes on how to approach a stranger on the subject of God, Jesus, church. He even found brochures that had been produced by other outreach programs, and one from a seminar he attended in Salt Lake City that year. He found other notes and pamphlets that he had read back then that someone else wrote. Daunted isn't even a word to explain his feelings at the moment. He kept on searching though, and after a while he tried to remember whether he kept notes on any specific churches he had contacted. Whether for ones who agreed to volunteer, or churches that didn't. He looked back in the filing cabinet to search for other possibilities, and found several other folders that might offer some help. One folder was named simply, *"things to do for City Outreach - 1999."* In that file were over a dozen sub folders each with a month and year hand written on them. He remembered doing that. His intention was to keep an up to date "to do" list for each month. He started to page through them, and found that only the first three months had anything recorded in them. Those folders did seem to be carefully organized with some notes on what he did to follow up on, but the rest of the folders were empty. He found another folder he had named *"Requests from Outreach Team."* And another named *"Names of Volunteers."* Another named *"Dates and Times.*" He remembered setting those folders up, way back then for when the team had planned to go out into the city. "*People in Need,*" "*Places in the City to Go,*" and then at last he found a folder, "*New Churches to Contact.*" That's it, he said, and he opened it. In there was a single sheet of paper with the names of different churches he had intended to talk to, and the church in question was listed there, but no notes for any one of those churches could be found. Mark looked up at the clock and saw that he had just spent the better part of two hours searching with no avail. "I know I kept notes on that church, I know I did. What would I have done with them?" He closed the filing cabinet drawers, and remembered why he stopped filing anything in there from about 2001 forward. That was when he started using his first computer, and all such notes, or information from then forward for the city outreach would be filed on his hard drive. But the only involvement he had ever had with "*that other church,*" was long before the birth of his new computer. He knew he would have no records for that church there.

He had a choice to make. Give up any search for his notes on the second of two churches he was contesting. "Contest," and that word stopped him in his tracks. "Hmmm...," his eyes opened a little wider. "Well, I suppose that's exactly what it is. I guess that's what I am doing," he had to admit, "it's a comparison between that other church and, and," he stammered mildly. "It's a comparison I am conducting between their church's ideology, and, and what? Ours? So, why am I needing to do that?" he asked himself. "AAAND?" He stopped to think, "and," he said again, "and I need to ask for advice from the only source known who always has the only correct answer. He prayed and asked for direction. He remembered Proverbs 3:5-6, *Trust in the Lord with all your heart, and lean not on your own understandings; In all your ways acknowledge Him, and He shall direct your path.* "Do you want me to pursue this search, and look for those notes? And if I find them, what do you want me to do with them, and what about this comparison, this contest I am conducting? Do you want me to just put that aside? Or should I just continue on with the job you gave me with Pastor Cambridge's journal?"

After some time, he felt it prudent to open up the journal again, and pick up where he left off with that, but he didn't. He couldn't shake the thought that this line of questioning about the differences between our two church's theologies was vital for him to figure out. Further he thought that the outcome of that side study had to have some major bearing on his work with the journal.

He took that as his direction on which of the two avenues he was to walk on. So, he started rummaging through his memory again, and prayed, to try and recall what he could have done with those notes. He did remember that he didn't keep too many notes on any one church at the time, whether they were for or indifferent to his City Outreach. "EXCEPT that church," he said plopping down in his recliner to yet once again rake his brain. Not only for what he did with the notes, but why, if they were so important, he didn't file them correctly. "Come on Marcus, think. Okay," he said, "I wasn't living here then, so what would I have done with them twenty or so years ago. I had a note book," he exclaimed, "and I wrote everything down in that, and I carried the notebook everywhere I went. I needed it with me at all times so I would know what was going on, and who was going to volunteer when, and I packed everything up when I moved here about six years ago, and I...I...I...I don't know. Did I even keep the notebook? Oh, it's hopeless," he said, a little disgusted with himself. "I probably threw it out after I started keeping all my notes on the computer, or maybe I just tossed the stupid notebook somewhere..." and Mark just stopped moving, but continued to talk out loud in slow motion... "like – in – the – trunk - of - my - car." He had only opened his car trunk a couple of times, ever. He never really used it, and every time he did open it in the last few years, he never investigated its contents. "Oh, my good gracious," he said, and don't you know, there it was. His old, hasn't been opened in who knows how many years, blue college ruled notebook. He brought it in, sat down heavily in his recliner, and began to page through it. He finally found one page that had been ear marked and he began to read...

June 14, 2000, Wednesday...Starbucks on Jefferson, Meeting with Mr. Kevin Stuart - Outreach Coordinator

"And I didn't go to their church. I met their representative at Starbucks. Maybe that's the reason I couldn't remember so much." But Mark just gazed at the title, they had given to their church. He remembered musing over that name then, as he was doing now. "Boy, that just about puts all the pieces of that puzzle together, doesn't it? That name tells it all," and just reading that brief little bit helped him to remember the outcome of that meeting. He continued to read in silence, but the memory of that meeting returned him to that point in time with extreme clarity. He remembered everything.

"WOW, that was the other church." Mark leaned back in his recliner, parked the notebook beside him on the floor, and just started to think what it all meant. "That church was, and is," he said out loud again, "a very large church. Who knows how many members, or attendees they have on any one Sunday morning?" Looking back, he could remember what their mission statement was, and what their main thrust of teaching was all about. Some of it sounded fairly biblical, but most all of the rest of it was off the charts, somewhere between a lost island in the Pacific and the moon. "I am equally sure that they haven't altered much since then either. The question I have always struggled with is, what am I, or any of us, supposed to do about it?" Mark recognized that he once again was making a comparison between that other church and his own church, and he knew that was not a good thing to do. The only comparison that should be made should only be made between God's Holy Word, and any church, including his own. He also knew that God is the righteous judge and that he certainly was "NOT," he accentuated. "BUT," he went on to say, "I really do know that, and I, from my heart, don't want to do that. I don't want to judge anyone, so why am I battling with this comparison…again?" He remembered back to when he first had that interview with their representative, and how the exact same battle was going on in his mind and his heart then.

Mark got up, looked down at the notebook he left on the floor, and commanded, "Stay," and then he laughed out loud for that moment staring at the notebook. "At least *you* know how to obey," he commented. "Lord," he said walking away, "help me to obey You in equal fashion." Then he began one of his most favorite things to do when unable to conclude a thought that he couldn't get rid of. He paced the floors of his house. He would walk from his living room into the kitchen and back again, taking a cruise through his office, where he would stop to gaze out of his window that looked out over the park across the street. Then back around again, talking to himself as if there were two of him, so as to create a debate.

"So," he began, "let me get a real grip on this comparison thing. What do you think, Marcus, is it fair to compare in the first place? And," he immediately brushed off the word fair, and went on to say "what am I really comparing with anyway?" Mark continued to converse with himself and pace for a short while. He knew what was **not** bothering him. He knew it was not the size of that, or any church for that matter, and he stopped to confess. "Size doesn't matter. I know of a couple of churches in the city, one of them very old, and both of them very large. I've visited those churches, talked in depth with their pastors, and their theology seems to be dead center accurate. Well, as far as I can see using the Bible as my guide. Oh," he reminded himself, "both of those churches are different denominations all together, so it isn't a denominational barrier I am comparing with either, on that other church. Certainly, there are some differences in some of the practices, and some traditions regarding almost every denomination, well that all of us face, but the bottom line of their basic doctrinal beliefs are almost one hundred percent agreeable. Pretty much the Nicene Creed covers it all. One God, the one true God spoken of in the Bible, one Jesus, the Name above all names, Savior of the entire human race who believe, and one Holy Spirit, and that all have sinned, and the only way to God is through Jesus...etc. Got it, and so do they, meaning churches who confess that Jesus is the only name by which one may be saved." Mark stopped in his office and sat down. After his debate with himself, he knew exactly what was causing this anguish he was having about that other church. He knew from the start, but what he had been struggling with was a two-fold dilemma. First was the fact that he was making this comparison, but now he concluded that he really wasn't making a comparison between his church and that other church. He was making a comparison between any other church and God's church, regardless of denomination or practices, or traditions, or anything, as long as "THAT CHURCH," meaning any church when it preached a different gospel than the one taught to us from the Bible.

He then asked himself a rhetorical question in reference to his second issue…, "Where does all this prayer and research lead, in regards to the journal that has been handed to me? How does making this comparison between any church, not just *that* one other church, and Your church, Lord, have to do with the outcome of my studying Pastor Jimmy Lee Cambridge's journal? Mark?" he said… "It sure does take you a while to catch on, doesn't it? I am struggling with myself," he finally decided, "but I needed to, so that I could know positively why it is important to make this kind of comparison, and secondly what it all has to do with the journal." Mark turned his computer on, and began to make some more notes. He opened his folder he started earlier on the journal and made a short list for himself to be accountable to while on this journey with Pastor's journal.

- Don't judge when make comparisons. Use any comparison only to better understand my walk with the Lord, and His Word, not someone else's.
- Don't look for faults to condemn. Look for correctness to teach.
- I need to use this example for the ultimate work God wants to do in me and our church.
- I see clearly what Pastor Cambridge finally saw when re-reading his own journal, so keep that in the front of your goals.
- Get rid of your discomfort and anger. Give all of it to God, and He will take it.
- I have been entrusted with a huge, not new, thing. It goes back to include the first teachings

that Jesus taught his disciples, and it is an easy task to do.

- THE BATTLE BELONGS TO THE LORD.

Mark picked up the phone and speed dialed Martha.

"Hello Mark," came her familiar voice. "I've been thinking about you. How's it going with the journal?

"That's why I called, to give you an update. It is going so good it's hard to describe."

"Anything special turn up for you?" she asked with just a bit of "I hope there is," attached to the attitude in her voice.

"Yeah, you could say that. But not actually something precisely out of the journal. Do you recall Pastor's entries he wrote when, I don't know their last names, but Greg and his wife Barb, along with Charles and Deborah left the church? He wrote that they said they wanted to find a church that taught about a God who fit more comfortably into their more modern life style?"

"Oh yes I do," Martha said with a slight attitude. "Yes, I do," she said a second time. "Boy, was that a hard time for all of us. It nearly broke Jimmy's heart. We did overcome that, though, and actually Jimmy told me a few years later that that one set of incidences was the root of him growing into becoming a most sought-after mentor and disciple maker. In fact, he said that it was because of that, that he had such a successful time mentoring you. Does that make any sense to you Mark?"

Mark couldn't help himself, and chuckled. "Sure does," he said.

"Care to share?" asked Martha.

"It's simple," Mark said, "because that is exactly what just happened to me. But that is a very long story, and I don't have time to go all the way through that now. Maybe we can have coffee again on Saturday, and I'll lay it all out on your table for you. How does that sound?"

"You got it. About ten again?"

"See you then, Martha," and he hung up waving his hand over his head like he always did, simply saying "Bye," but he said that after he had hung up.

Mark opened the journal, and raised a hand in the air like it was an antenna for God to touch. "Okay, Marcus" …

But You
The Journal

4

Significance

… **"Okay, Marcus,"**

He began to dig deeper into that first journal. Marcus was his birth name, and what he called himself whenever he was really ready to knuckle down to tackle some very serious project, **"keep reading**." And so, he did. He finished the fourth journal several months later, keeping excellent notes so that he could confer with Martha. He did call and talk with her on occasion to give her an update, and even visited with her after church sometimes to discuss one entry or another, and to gain some more information about some particular point that the pastor referred to. But he finally completed what Pastor Jimmy Lee Cambridge had to say about forty-some years of ministry. He had read every one of his entries, every extra notation and every Scripture reference his beloved old pastor had recorded.

Cindy Can't Be Trusted with Holding a Kid's Popsicle

"Ok, Martha, I'm done," Mark announced when she answered the phone. "I finished last Friday night late, and spent all last Saturday mulling over all my notes, but I'm ready to meet with you. How does Saturday at ten again sound to you?"

"Saturday mornings are always open, sounds great, Mark, I'll have the coffee on," she said with a mildly disguised anxious tone in her voice. "I am ready to listen to what you have to share."

Saturday took longer to show up than he would have liked, but Mark packed the four journals back into the canvas tote they came in, along with a small notebook of his hand written comments, and set off for Martha's house.

When she opened the door, he was surprised to see three other ladies from their church there to greet him. Of course he knew all of them, and treated them with respect and kindness, but he could not pretend to be glad to see them there.

"I know you didn't know we were going to be here," Kendra York said, stepping forward when Mark entered the foyer, "but we have all been keeping tabs on you via Martha since she gave you Pastor Jimmy's journal." Mark said nothing at all. "Well," she continued, "we, ah, didn't even know he kept a journal," she laughed nervously turning her head toward Cindy for support, "did we Cindy?"

Cindy nodded with an affirmative glance, looked up at Mark, "Oh, yeah, and we're all interested. I hope that's okay."

Mark shot a quick glance to Martha for some kind of explanation, but recognized the same disguised confused look on her face that he probably was demonstrating on his own.

The silence that fell across the room when Mark didn't answer immediately said more than anything he could have affirmed or denied. But after a short moment, he responded. "Sure, ah yeah, sure it's okay." But after that let's call it a long enough pause to drive a truck through, it left an awkward, *what*, in all their thoughts. "Well," Martha blurted out to save the day, "I've got some goodies to eat and we have a fresh pot of coffee. Let's all go into the living room. Much more comfortable in there. You all get seated and I'll serve. Ah, Kendra will you help?"

Mark sat down and waited for Cindy and Gracie to come in and get comfortable. They all sat down and were waiting for Kendra and Martha to join them. The silence continued for a couple of more minutes until Cindy abruptly pursed out an elongated, "SOOO, what are we talking about here, Mark? You and Pastor Jimmy were always so close. Did you get something from his journal that we all need to know about?"

Mark kindly looked first at Cindy then at Gracie, and finally said. "You know, there is nothing at all in Pastor's journal that either one of you two could not read. There are no secrets here, no additional items mentioned, or persons mentioned or anything recorded that any one, or even both of you would not benefit from. There weren't even any instructions that he wrote about. It is just a simple journal, actually four journals, that Pastor Cambridge kept for almost forty years. Sermon notes, prayer requests etc. Just his personal notes. That's all there is to that."

Cindy and Gracie kind of mildly rolled their eyes, and then Cindy said, "And all we get is, what, what do we get, that's all there is to that?"

"I don't know what you were expecting," Mark said nonchalantly. "I was gifted with these notebooks from Pastor, and asked to read them, and then evaluate for myself what I should or should not do with any information that I was to discover from it."

"Annnnnd?" came a harmonized response from the two ladies simultaneously, "what information do you have that you could share with us?" Cindy finished.

"Annnnnd," Mark said in a kind of mocking way, "that is what I did. I came here out of respect for Martha to share with her what I thought about her husband's journal. Annnnnd," he elongated the word again, "that's it." Mark was kind enough in the way he presented his statement, but also, he said it in a "that settles that," kind of way. "I do have some thoughts that I will be wanting to share with our new pastor later, but that will be when I can meet with him. Last Sunday was his first, and I expect that he will be rather busy settling in."

"Why can't you share with us, now?" Cindy pushed the issue again.

"I tell you the truth," Mark confirmed the second time, "there is nothing here at all that I could not share with anyone, but there will come a time when I will share with all of you what outcome I have concluded from Pastor's decades of notes, but not today. Not until I have had a chance to have a *private* meeting with Martha about her husband's journal. You should respect that, and after that, with our new pastor and all the elders." And, right at that moment they all jumped at least an inch off of their chairs at the unmistakable sound of Martha yelling loud enough to wake the dead… "**NOOOO**," from the kitchen.

A storm had been brewing in the kitchen while the rest of them were having their discussion in the living room. "Kendra York," Martha scolded, "what in the name of common sense are you doing? I told you about that journal just in passing only a week after Jimmy was buried. I was hurting, you knew that, and I needed someone to talk with, and you promised to keep that just between us."

"I know, I know," Kendra said in a pitiful kind of voice, "and I'm so sorry. I let it slip to Cindy, and…"

"And what?" Martha bellowed the words almost inaudibly for only Kendra's ears to hear through her clenched teeth. "Cindy can't be trusted with holding a kid's popsicle. What were you thinking? And you know that Gracie isn't any better. Did you also tell them about the other times that I mentioned to you that Mark was dropping by when he did? And now, the three of you gossipers show up on my doorstep just minutes before Mark, *u n I n v I t e d*," she elongated the word for effect, "you, you…you told them he was coming today, didn't you, and at what time. I told you that the other day because you wanted to go shopping, and I couldn't go, and I told you why. Another thing I want to know is what on earth did you tell Cindy and Gracie about that journal in the first place? Wait a minute," and Martha paused, "I didn't tell you anything about Jimmy's journal at all, except to say that Mark had finished it last week, and would be coming here this morning…" she suddenly stopped talking with her gestured hands frozen, just hanging there in the air, a look of total shock on her face and bulging eyes that could have burned holes through Kendra's brain. "So," she continued, "this morning you three just show up one minute before Mark and, what? Hello? Surprise?"

"I'm so sorry, Martha," Kendra said again, "I really am. I'll make it right," and she stepped sideways to pass Martha, and was about to slide into the living room.

Martha cut her off like a linebacker for the Packers… "**NOOOO**," Martha yelled at the top of her voice, "I will, and she turned on her heel and stomped into the other room.

"Okay, ladies, I got the picture. Kendra has been my friend for maybe thirty years, and you, Gracie, longer than that. The two of you ladies have totally stepped over the line. And you, Cindy," turning her glare directly to her face, "are no better. I have befriended each and every one of you for decades. I have, until today, never raised my voice to any of you. I have always opened my house, and my heart to you all, but this," she stammered for the right words, and couldn't find any, "this," she said again, and made a deliberated effort to calm down and lower her voice. "This," she said the third time, "is, well, it's way out of bounds. You still are always welcome here, and you don't even need to call first. I guess that is what you did today, but you do need to show some manners, some respect, and some maturity," and that last word found her angry voice again. "You can't gather information from me and just show up because you want to know what's going on. Now, I am asking you to leave." Kendra started to say something, but was cut off, "NOW!" Martha exclaimed bringing both her hands up over her head gesturing that she was not interested in hearing anything from any of them. That got the point, and they were all gone in less time than it took for the dust to settle.

Be On Your Guard

Martha slumped down in a chair, covered her eyes with her hands, and just sobbed. "I am so sorry, Mark. I didn't reveal anything at all to Kendra, or either of the other two. Whatever they think they know; they have made up themselves. I am so sorry."

"There is no need to be sorry. None what-so-ever. There is nothing for them to know anyway. What happened here today is just a small example of what Pastor was wanting me to come up with, and it was written right there between the lines of his forty years of journaling. I am calling that journal he gifted me with my 'rite of passage'. Now, here's something to think about. The real gift Pastor Jimmy left will mostly be for those three ladies and others, men and women alike just like them, if they will listen and learn. It has nothing to do with gossiping either. What do you think, Martha, what do you think

Pastor would say to each of them right at this moment, were he hear to do so?"

"You got to love them, Marty," she said through burning eyes. "He would simply say 'you just got to love them.' And you know what?" she continued. "He would. He would not let it slide and he would confront each one of them, but he would love them anyway. He certainly would."

"And so will we. I have so much to share with you about his journals, but," and at that Mark remembered that she had been a part of it and Pastor all those years. She was fully aware of what he was going to come up with. "Tell you what," Mark shifted gears and said, "let's wait on that for another time. My first move, anyway, should be to spend some real quality time with our new pastor and hopefully lean on him for some sound advice. Then I can have a meeting with him and the elders together. I think," he went on, "it would be extremely profitable for you to be there as well as the pastor's wife and the elder's wives as well."

Martha became calm, stood up, and said, "You know, you would have made a great pastor yourself. Want some coffee?"

"No, I wouldn't have made a great pastor," he sang, "and you know why. I don't have the patience. But you bet I'd like some coffee."

"You demonstrated patience right here, that pastor-kind- of-patience," she said. "But Mark, you have changed it seems, if this is the new you. I remember not that long ago when you had a great deal of difficulty meting out patience. Either way, Jimmy would have been proud of you."

"You know Martha, remember just now when I said I named Pastor's journal my 'rite of passage'? Well, that is just one of the benefits that came from reading it. Patience like I've never known before, but I promise you, if I had to pastor a church? Well, let's just say, they, whoever they are, are glad that I am not. There is one more thing, though," Mark began but paused.

"What is it, Mark?" she asked. "Something else wrong?"

"No, no, nothing wrong, I, ah, well there was one entry, the last entry in the journal that he wrote. And I didn't read it. I started to, but when I saw that he was addressing that last message directly to me, I kind of froze. I noticed, also, that it was not written in his hand, so I stopped reading. I discerned that it had to be very personal, and that it must have been your hand writing." Mark stammered through a short pause as if a little embarrassed. "Can we read that together?"

Martha patted Mark on the hand. "I would love to do that for you, kiddo. I would love to do that. And you're right, it is my note that I wrote for him. He told me what to write. Let's get some coffee, and we'll take a look at it."

They went into her kitchen, got their coffee, and pulled up a chair. Mark opened the journal to the last page and Martha started to read, but had to stop for the tears. Actually, they both had to gain their composure. The words written there seemed to sound like Pastor Jimmy was there reading it to them, and they had to restart multiple times. Finally, they both took a deep breath, cleared their throats, kind of chuckled at each other, and went on.

April 2021

These four journals are for you, Mark. I didn't write them for you, I didn't write any of them for anyone, really, but I see that they have to come to you. I began writing my first year at seminary, but I removed all those notes. They don't apply. I kept writing almost every Sunday since. Most all of what I wrote about ended up pretty generic, but there were some really inspired entries, and I know you will find them. Those are the ones you'll need to sort through. Certainly, I cannot tell now, nor am I worried about what you will find, and what you will do about what you read. I faithfully trust God for all of this, and for you, my dear son in the faith. I have no doubt that you will know precisely what to do with all that you read here. There's a lot of heart on these pages, Mark, but I pass it on to you in much the same way I imagine Paul passed it on to Timothy in his last letter before he was executed for his crime of spreading the good news that Jesus is the risen Son of God. I could end with, "God be with you," but I know that He already is. So, I'll close with this, "I'll be seeing you sometime later."

My final note, Mark...Be on your guard. God's truth, God's Word, and God's reality are on trial now, and it's up for the taking. And when things close in on you, remember what Paul said to his true son in the faith. He wrote to Timothy, but you, oh man of God, you be different.

They finished their coffee in silence. Neither one of them was able to speak, and it took them a while to pull themselves together. Finally, Mark stood and told Martha that she had been a rock for her Jimmy, "Well, for all of us, really," Mark confided. So, Mark, waving his hand over his shoulder like he always did, letting go with his signature single word, "Bye," started home to figure out what his next best move was going to be with the journal.

_____

_____

But You
The Journal
5
Unveiled

We Just Ignore It

Mark was deep in thought on his ride home from Martha's, but not about the disruption he encountered from those wonderful busy-body ladies from church. He was consumed by how he was going to follow through with the journals. When he walked into his office, he pulled the four notebooks from the tote and casually stacked them on the seat of one of his side chairs. He dropped his note pad down, onto the center of his desk top. He momentarily ogled his notes, and then spoke out loud to them. "Hmmm, how do I proceed with you now?" and it sounded like a prayer, but it wasn't. It was him simply talking out loud to himself. "Well," he corrected his last blatant remark, "really, Lord, I need your help to know how to proceed." He took his gaze off his notes, for his thoughts moved to a more immediate concern. He was hungry, so he exchanged his dilemma in the office for a sandwich and a glass of milk in the kitchen. He chewed on more than his sandwich for lunch, though. When he had finished, he got up, put his dishes in the sink and sat back down with that identifiable crease across his forehead. He continued to evaluate how to jump off this, *I don't know exactly how to do what I know I have to do next,* cliff that had been handed to him. After some time, he got up and went into his office to mull over all the notes he had taken for the last few months in an attempt to gain a better perspective on how to move forward most effectively. He picked up his notepad, and opened his center desk drawer looking for something to write with. His idea was to get settled comfortably in his living room recliner, and leisurely read and make some more notes, but there was no pen in that drawer. "Am I a lousy secretary, or what," he said again out loud. "I must have several dozen pens, and can I find one when I need one? Nooo, of course not," and with that he opened a couple of other drawers in his desk but not one pen was to be found. Finally, he opened the last drawer. He was sure there was no pen in there, because he only used it for storage, but out of frustration and a lack of anywhere else to look he pulled the drawer open. Instantly he was taken back to another place and time. He didn't pick it up at first, but just stared at it. Then, slowly, he lifted the large old black Bible from its resting place and gently put it on his desk. He sat down, discarded his notepad, and ran his hands across this old relic of a memory. He had forgotten that it was even in there, and couldn't remember the last time he even looked at it. His facial expression exhibited both joy for the remembrance that embraced his love language, and pain for the remembrance that embraced his life's worst experiences. When he got this old Bible, he remembered, it was in a wreck of a mess. He paid a large sum of money to have it re-conditioned, and re-bound, and took extra caution to preserve the pages with all the personal hand written notes that were left for him to read.

"There it is," he said, "there it all is, isn't it? We look at that book, we know what that book is, we know that it holds unbending truths, and we just ignore it, sometimes, don't we? We are drawn to it when we want proof that we aren't so bad having God's grace, and we're drawn to it when we know that we are so bad, whether we have God's grace or not. We quote it to prove some ideal we believe in, even if our wisdom is telling us, down deep, that we know we are wrong. We quote it to someone else when we want to prove that they are wrong, or rebelliously out of bounds with God. But," and Mark lightened up a bit, "we won't receive any correction from anyone else when they use that book to prove something pertaining to us, will we? We pray that we will be satisfied when we are being accused of something, whether we did it or not. We look for hope from this book we say we believe in, but in truth our actions, sometimes, don't reflect our belief, do they? Why is it that, so often, a hand grenade needs to go off right in our lap before we fear the outcome of our life based on the truth of God's Word, more than contemplating tomorrow's two-piece chicken dinner?"

Mark looked up from his preach he was presenting to his office walls and laughed at himself. "Look at me," he said, "here I am, all alone and talking to myself again. Correction," he said, "talking to the walls." He threw his hands up in frustration, and brought them back down with a slap against his thighs. "Well, I guess I should be thankful that the walls aren't educated enough to talk back."

He turned his attention back to that Bible. Initially it was purchased by his grandmother. Her name and that first date recorded in the front, read, *Betty Kiley, Bible purchased June 14, 1937.* Many more entries were made that same day, Mark believed, because the penmanship was the same, with the same color ink that looked like it came from the same pen. His grandfather's name and all their birth dates, marriages, other names of cousins, aunts and uncles, etc. "That's an exercise that most people don't do any more." He read about his mom and dad's marriage, and the deaths of relatives he never heard of. There must have been several dozen more entries with dates recorded over time up to the last date grandma penned. She wrote. *April 3, 1963. Bible passed to my daughter, Judith L. Kiley Garner.* "So," Mark thought, "Mom got this after they were married." But he noticed that there were only two more entries, total, listed after that and they seemed to be from his mom's hand recording. Mark paused, and then in just a couple of decibels louder than a whisper, "It's our birth dates, Shelly and me." as he ran his hand across the names. He remembered reading all this before, but it had been so long ago. Shelly was his sister, but he never found out what happened to her.

His mind jumped to all the memories of him and his family. Mark's father and mother divorced when he was only twelve, his sister would have been eight. Mark remembered that dad would come by on holidays and their birthdays, but only for that first year, and then he just disappeared. Mom sank into major depression, not being able to care for us kids, was hospitalized first for that and then a year later, twice, for drug overdose. Child Protective Services stepped in and took us away, he recalled. We were farmed out to several different homes, and none of them worked. "Well, they didn't work for me," he said out loud again. "I don't think that they worked out for Shelly either. I don't know." He was sixteen when he ran away, and they never caught up with him until he was arrested in New Jersey for burglary at the age of twenty-three. The court was lenient on him, but it did bring him to the realization that he could not be a criminal, and find any lasting joy. So, he went back to see what ever happened to his family. Mom had committed the final act of depression, by taking her own life via an overdose of heroine. He tried desperately to find out what ever happened to his sister, but it seemed that it was to become and stay a secret. Mark continued to flounder for the next eight years, until that one fateful day when he wondered into Pastor Jimmy Lee Cambridge's church, and God turned his life eternally around.

"Wow, I tell you what, WOW!" Mark shook himself loose from those old memories. Memories that Pastor Jimmy had spent almost a year helping him to overcome. "Traps," he used to call them, and on one occasion he called them death traps. "Mark," he said, "you are not guilty of anything in your past, if in fact you have received forgiveness for your sins through Christ, and you have. God has forgiven you because of your confession, and because of your faith in Jesus. God doesn't hold anything against you at all." Mark remembers Pastor going on with, "You are set free, Mark. Say it." Mark chuckled at that memory, He remembered just looking at Pastor back then and thinking, "Well, I can say it, but I don't have to," and he chuckled again at the thought of how often Pastor would accuse Mark of just being stubborn. "Say it," Pastor would show his stubborn side as well by not giving up, "say, I am set free from even the guilt of my sin," Pastor would not let up on him. "Come on," Pastor would beg, "Mark, you need to say it." Mark remembered finally giving in and saying it, but it wasn't loud enough to satisfy Pastor. "SAY IT," Pastor demanded, and just an instant later, Pastor encouraged him again, "Mark, I'm telling you, it will really help you, just say it." Mark sat there in his office now, some twenty plus years later, reminiscing that time with his marvelous mentor, and spoke those words again, like he finally did back then. He said them out loud to the walls with a tear in his eye. "You know what Pastor? You were right on the money even way back then, and you're right now." Mark could not hold back the laughter, though, in spite of his tears, when he leaned his head back and yelled just loud enough to not disturb any neighbors, "I am set free from even the guilt of my sin, and it helps even now. Thank you, Lord, and thank you Pastor Jimmy." His laughter subsided to a quiet personal think tank mood and he softly mouthed, "I sure wish you were here

to help me figure out how to move forward with your journal."
And he fell silent for one imaginary moment pretending to hear
his old pastor speak to him. "Yeah, I know," Mark confessed,
and not for the last time, "it's my turn to figure things out now,
isn't it?"

Still holding the Bible, he remembered how it came to
him in the first place. It was in a box that was kept by one of
Mom's next-door neighbors, who gave it to Mark when he
showed up after coming back from New Jersey. He had gone
back to his mother's old apartment hoping to get some
information about her, and that led him to the neighbor. She
had lived there nearly her whole life. He remembered that she
and Mom had been friends. She remembered him and Shelly
before the two of them were sent off to different foster homes.
She told Mark what had happened to his mother, but that she
didn't know what ever happened to Shelly. She was happy to
give Mark the box. "This is all there is from her," she said.
"Everything else that was in her apartment was taken away to
Goodwill, or somewhere. This box was left behind on her
porch, I think by accident, so I picked it up and kept it for, well,
maybe for you. No one ever came by to check on her, or to find
out what became of her until now."

Mark didn't even look through the box for those nine
years before he found Pastor Cambridge's church. It must have
been within that first few months of Mark being mentored, that
he told the pastor about the box he was given, but never wanted
to open it. He was encouraged to do so, and when he did, along
with some cookbooks, and a couple of cheap pieces of jewelry,

was this Bible. He showed it to Pastor, and he was advised to have it re-conditioned, so he did. But during that process he was introduced to all those hand written notes that his grandmother had penned.

Mark closed the Bible, and was ready to put it back in the drawer, when he remembered something else he had discovered back when he had it re-bound. He anxiously flung the Bible open again to the last pages at the back of the Bible to reveal several more hand written memos. "Probably written by Grandma," he surmised. He didn't have a clue what they all meant when he first found them, over twenty years before, but he clearly got the message now. He read her notes as if it was the first time…

…I am writing this to you in hopes that you will discover the real love of God through Christ the way that I have. The words in this Bible are just as real and true as anything you will ever encounter. I have already prayed this for you, and hope that these scriptures will help you find what you are looking for.

It just stared out like that. There was no mention as to who it was written for, but Mark presumed that Grandma was writing it to his mother. It didn't matter though; Mark took them for himself. After that short note, there were several Scriptures that she took the time to write out.

"Trust in the Lord with all your heart, and lean not on your own understandings, in all your ways acknowledge Him, and He will direct your paths." Prov 3:5-6

"You could use that right now, couldn't you Marcus," he breathed quietly to himself.

"How then shall they call on Him in whom they have not believed? And how shall they believe in Him of whom they have not heard? And how shall they hear without a preacher? And how shall they preach unless they are sent? As it is written: "How beautiful are they feet of those who preach the gospel of peace, who bring glad tidings of good things." - Romans 10:14-15

"Then He said to them all, "If anyone desires to come after Me, let him deny himself, and take up his cross daily, and follow Me." For whoever desires to save his life will lose it, but whoever loses his life for My sake will save it." - Luke 9:23-24

"And that," Mark said, "is where I will need to pull some band aids off of some wounds," referring to what he was to do with Pastor Cambridge's journal.

"Then Jesus said to those Jews who believed Him, "If you abide in My word, you are My disciples indeed. And you shall

know the truth, and the truth shall make you free." - John 8:31-32

"And, ditto with the band aids again," he said. "Those seemed to be odd Scriptures to share with Mom," he thought, "but maybe they were meant for someone else. Maybe they weren't meant for anyone, but only for her own edification, or," and he reasoned, "maybe they were simply, unbeknownst to her, meant for me. Doesn't matter, I'll take them, and thank you God for this reminder of your Word, and your direction."

Mark just sat there consumed in awe of how God works. "You do work in wondrous ways, don't you, Lord." He closed the Bible again, staring at it, wondered who on earth would want to have it when he was gone. He opened his storage drawer and reverently placed the Bible back in its resting place, and mentally noted that, "this wasn't an accident, was it Lord?"

"Mark," he stated as a matter of fact, "this is just what you needed," and continued with, "who are any of us, if not Yours to guide, and why should any of us imagine that we might be in the wrong place and time, instead of imagining that we are in the right place and time, if in fact we have offered up our hearts for you to use as You wish, for Your glory? And yes, that is my prayer." He thanked God again for always providing an answer, and for his old mentor, friend and pastor.

Mark realized that through this last hour of reminiscing, he had been given the answer he was needing. He wanted to call the new pastor to set up a meeting, but thought it wiser to wait at least a week, or more maybe, to give him more time to settle in.

But You

The Journal

6

Revealed

Trust in the Lord with Only Part of Your Heart?

The next week found Mark researching all his notes again just to be well prepared when he did meet with the pastor. He wanted to make sure all the elders were there as well. He had no doubt that at least two of the elders, Randy and Chris, would have no trouble with what he wanted to present. He had discipled both of them for a couple of years after his eight years on the elder board. He waited until Tuesday after their Sunday service the following week, and picked up his phone and called his new pastor, and waited for Pastor Abraham Bleeker to pick up.

"You have reached Pastor Abraham Bleeker. Please leave a…" "Hello, Pastor Bleeker," he announced. "What may I do for you today?"

"Well, hello to you too, Pastor, not sure you will remember me, my name is Mark Garner."

"Yes, I do remember you. What can I do for you?" he said again.

"I imagine that you are still settling in, but I would like to schedule an appointment with you to discuss something very important. I have spent the last few months reading a..."

"Journal," Pastor finished his sentence. "I know about the journal."

Silence followed, and then finally Mark questioned. "Okay, I assume you have been talking with Martha?"

"Well yes I have, but actually, 'I heard it through the grape vine...'" and he sang it in a kind of comic imitation of The Pips' recording of the song from the sixties.

"Really," Mark retorted, "and first of all, that song was recorded, what, some twenty years before you were born?" He questioned. "Do you like old music like that?"

"Not really," Pastor admitted. "My mother used to sing that to us whenever she wanted to teach us kids about gossiping."

"That's cute. Maybe I'll steal that line and use it myself sometime," Mark thought. "Well," he said, "what I am looking for is to have a meeting with you about that journal, and there are four of them that collectively span forty years of journaling. Can I ask you what you heard about it?"

"Let me put your thoughts at ease, Mark," Pastor started off. A little over a week ago, after my first Sunday, I called all the elders together asking them to give me as much information about your church, and more specifically, your church's congregation as they could. The District had already given me all of the background they had, but I wanted a first-hand look at the general week to week ministry that would be needed here. By the way, it appears from District's point of view, that little to no conflict ever comes from this church. I know that makes them happy. Anyway, I have learned many things as a result of that meeting with the elders. Much about how and when the church was started. All the outreaches we have. The names of those in need currently for a variety of reasons, and just how much all of you loved Pastor Cambridge. I also learned, Mr. Mark Garner," he said in a complementary tone, "about you. I learned that you were an elder here yourself for, I think it was eight years. They did tell me that you were very close to Pastor Cambridge. I understand that he personally mentored you, and that you are our lay leader. I also learned that you mentored two of our elders, Randy and Chris, for a couple of years and then stepped down as elder to devote more time to our City Outreach, and that has been, what, a dozen years ago now?" Pastor Bleeker waited for an answer from Mark.

"Well, yes, that sounds about right, is there a question in there?" Mark asked.

"No, I just want you to know that I have been trying to do my homework."

"You and Pastor Jimmy would have gotten along just fine. He was like that too. In fact, it was sometimes uncanny how he seemed to always be informed."

"Let me get back to how and what I heard about your journal," Pastor Bleeker continued. "I first heard about it via those three ladies in question, and of course after that I did call Martha to gain not only information about the journal, but also about our three ladies. She dialed me into your meeting with them at her house. I was approached by those three together and they didn't really tell me much at all. I think their hearts were in the right place because it seemed like they just wanted to inform me that you had a journal that Pastor Cambridge wrote, so they're just fine. I can't call it gossip, but I could see gossip on their faces had I pursued the point further with them. As it was, I just thanked them and that closed the door on the journal topic with them. That was about it."

"I don't know how much you learned from Martha, but I feel, and I believe so does she, that we need to get together and discuss what I have discovered. Would you be willing to do that?"

"Sure, and Martha already prepared me for your request. In addition, I think that we should have the elders here, and all our wives as well," Pastor Bleeker bounced it back off of Mark.

"Ah, yeah," Mark kind of stuttered. "I was going to ask you for that. Don't tell me you are some kind of mind reader also?"

"Not at all. It was Martha's suggestion, and she did fill me in some about Pastor Cambridge's journaling. How he kept it for forty years, how he would write in it every Sunday after church and so on, but she did tell me, also, that it was you who needed to present your finding, and that it would be *most advisable,* she put it, if I would allow this meeting to take place and soon. So, how does this Thursday fit with your schedule. Say around seven?"

"Actually, that's perfect. "Mark said.

"Yeah, I was hoping that would work. I already had a meeting scheduled with the elders that night just to get things started here at the church, so I know all of them will be here. I will invite all our wives as well, and most likely they will come. I will line up someone who could come and watch their children, if they need that, and Martha already told me that she was keeping all her evenings open so that whenever we were to have the meeting, she will be free to come as well. So, I'll see you Thursday evening at seven."

"Thanks Pastor," Mark sounded very thankful. "I will be looking forward to telling you what I have learned." Mark hung up the phone having a really good feeling about his new pastor.

All day Wednesday and Wednesday night sped by Mark very slowly. His mind would race, but his clock did not. "Tick tock," he found himself jokingly saying to himself late Wednesday night way into the early hours of Thursday, "tick-tock," and then he got up out of his recliner, and was going to go over his notes yet again, but stopped. "Oh, come on, Mark," he thought, "did you get anything out of that Scripture Grandma left for you? How does that read again?" he asked himself. "Oh yeah…Trust in the Lord with only part of your heart? - NOT! Rely on some of your understandings? NOT! In

83

some of your ways acknowledge Him? NOT! And He might direct your path? NOT! So," he finally conceded to himself, "go to bed." And he did. He had to get up early for work, having had only a few hours sleep, but he felt renewed and refreshed anyway. He carried no worries at all about his presentation he was to give that evening with the pastor and elders, and he chuckled often because he found himself whistling that famous tune that came out of Snow White. "Hi-ho, hi-ho, it's off to work I go..." and he would start to laugh each time it came to mind. "You are good, God," he would follow up with, "You are so good."

Mark's peace came abundantly to him, because he felt that he knew exactly what, how and why he was to present what he had to present. He knew it would be very controversial. He also knew just how absolutely critical it would be to not hold back on anything he wanted to bring to the surface. "Controversial," he thought, "because there are many people in our current cultural structure who don't, can't, or won't see just how far out of bounds our society, at large, has become compared to the truth of God's Word. And," he continued, "absolutely critical to bring these truths to bear, because there are so many in our Christian communities who don't, can't, or won't see just how far out of bounds so many in our churches, even some of our church leaders, have become compared to the truth of God's Word. Boy, that's a mouthful," he thought. Those same thoughts had come to him often in the last few months, and even up until he was reminded of God's perfect timing and truths. So, he was prepared for tonight.

Mark showed up a little early, and was greeted by Pastor Bleeker and his wife, Barbara.

"Glad we can get together tonight," he said to Mark. "I'm looking forward to what you have to share with us."

He was given a cup of coffee, and they waited for the others to show up. "Are all the wives able to make it?" Mark asked.

"Yes, they are," Barbara answered, and they just small talked for a minute or two and then Barbara jumped up to greet Martha. "Good to see you."

"It's good to be seen," Martha said kindly. "Are you settling in ok? Is there anything you need? Is there anything I can do to help?"

"We're disorganized, but that won't last long. I hope we can serve your congregation as well as you and Pastor Cambridge did. I know we are stepping into some very large boots, but we will do our best."

"My Jimmy and I started this church, but it looks like you and Pastor Abraham will do just fine." Martha looked down at Mark and smiled, "I only wish we would find a she to come long side this one."

"Probably won't happen," Mark said shaking his head from side to side. "I'm just a couple of years shy of sixty. Who would want me now?"

"Mark," Barbara said, "you want us to look for you?"

"Not on your life," Mark emphatically stated. "I am not interested, and please that is not a call for you ladies to make it your next best adventure. Besides, I am very busy."

The rest of the elders and their wives showed up, and after a few minutes of greetings Pastor announced that they should get started. They all sat down, except for Mark. He saw that the pastor had provided a podium for him, but he deliberately picked it up and set it to the side. He then stepped forward to be closer to them all. As opposed to speaking at them, he wanted to have them feel like he was speaking with them. When all was quiet, he lowered his head and very quietly, very gently, began to pray. He didn't even announce, "Let's pray," he just prayed. After he was finished, he looked up at them, but didn't say a word, knowing that probably all of them were wondering what Mark was going to do, or what any of them were supposed to do. "Be still and know that I am God," he finally said. "I'll teach you all a poem I heard once about that sometime."

He began, "All of you, I assume, know about Pastor Cambridge's journal by now, but in case you didn't know, he didn't have a journal, he actually had four of them. Each is dated for a ten-year period, so his journals, or notebooks date back a little over forty years. It started out with only him and Martha knowing about his journaling, but then shortly after God took Pastor home, Martha dialed me into this. I have no idea what you have heard about the journals, or who said what, but here's the truth," and Mark conveyed all that had transpired from the time he had been given the journals to this night when they were all meeting.

"Let me start by telling you this. There is nothing, and I will repeat, nothing in all of Pastor's writings, from his very first set of notes, over forty years ago to the last few entries he penned several months ago now, that would even give us a hint of any kind, in reference to what I am charged with bringing to you tonight." Mark paused for a longer than necessary moment to allow that statement to really sink in. "There were no instructions, no secrets, no statements of encouragement, discouragement or admonishment for the church, Martha, me, or anyone else. There wasn't even a mention, in any of his notes, that would bring me to this point of understanding. There was not one entry, ever, that gave any information, or even a reference to look out for anything. There was nothing he wrote, nothing at all, in and of itself," and he emphasized *in and of itself*, "that would entice anyone to want to look any further for any additional information. It was simply his personal journaling. They were Pastor Cambridge's private notes meant to be viewed by only Pastor Cambridge. If I was to simply read his journals for the sole purpose of reminiscing my relationship with the man who mentored and discipled me, we might not be here tonight. Without the assignment I was given, I would just thank God for the opportunity to be reminded of the dedicated man I was privileged to call my pastor." Mark paused for effect again, and then finished with, "it's just one man's private journaling."

They all glanced around the room at each other briefly, and then Pastor Bleeker was the first to open up by simply stating the obvious. "Okay, if there was nothing to be gained from reading his journals, why are we all here? It seems that he would certainly have had some purpose for wanting to leave his journals behind to investigate."

"I didn't say that there was nothing to be gained," Mark corrected. "Obviously I have learned much from his journals that *can* end up being a major turning point in all our ministries. Reading Pastor Cambridge's journal with that added assignment of what to look for, offered up a life time of eye-opening information. And with that for my guide to study as I read, instead of simply reading it for nostalgic purposes, left me awestruck for why *we* literally have allowed the wool to be pulled over our eyes for so long. And the *"we"* I am referring to is not just us here in this room, or only our church. "We," means some parts of many church leaderships, and a high number of parishioners in probably all churches."

"Let me back up a moment. When I said that there was nothing he wrote, in and of itself, that would dial anyone into seeing what I am about to share with you, I meant it. It was actually what wasn't written in his journals that woke me up. In all of the almost forty years of him journaling, he wrote nothing that anyone could get some divine meaning from, other than the sermon messages, and some other notes Pastor Cambridge wrote about. Even he himself didn't see what I am about to share with you until he re-read his own journals several months ago now. It became clear to him then, and that is when he instructed Martha to give me his journals after he was gone. You'll remember that he was unable to fill the pulpit for, what maybe a year, prior to his last days, and," Mark stopped mid-sentence, and turned to Martha. "Martha, maybe this would be a good time for you to share what transpired between Pastor and you concerning his journals."

Martha turned slightly in her chair so as to address them all. "Jimmy has been journaling all his life, well from his first year in seminary. I didn't even know about it for a while, but he just seemed to want to do that. I knew he would take maybe a half an hour after every Sunday service, go alone into the den, and scribble his notes in the journal, and then we would eat lunch. He did that faithfully, every week all those years. Even up until he could not fill the pulpit anymore. After he was diagnosed with bone cancer, he started taking some treatments, but in the end, he decided that he would rather just leave it all up to God for the timing. It wasn't long then until we were told that there was no hope, and that he was terminal. As you all know, he was unable to stand well enough to hold Sunday services. That's when District started sending us interim pastors, and Jimmy and I just stayed at home. Most of those pastors, and all of you elders as well, and the ladies of the church never stopped visiting, bringing us meals and such, but Jimmy was getting more and more tired, and bored I might add. He found himself mentally alert, but unable to do anything else at all. It must have been about four months prior to him leaving us, that he called me in to his room to, "You've got to get a hold of this," he said. He told me that he had been reading his journals from the beginning, and shared with me what he thought about all the years of his writings, and gave me his instructions of what he wanted me to do with all his notebooks after he, well after he died. He made it clear that he wanted

Mark to have all of his writings, and to derive whatever he was to come up with, and don't you know... Mark came up with the exact same thing that Jimmy and I did." She turned back around to face Mark again and said, "Okay, kiddo, it's up to you now."

"Hmmm," Mark thought, "I've heard that before coming out of my own mouth," but brushed it off. "You need to clearly understand," Mark continued, "and I'll say this yet again. It's not what Pastor Cambridge wrote in his journals that jumped out at me like a sore thumb. It's what was not written that simply existed there between all the lines. It was totally unintentional, for sure, but there it was, and it bounced out at me, well at Pastor Jimmy first, with a kind of epiphany, that brought a heart throbbing, "Are you kidding me?" line of questioning to the surface. That, then, is what led me to bring to you all of what I have discovered. Now, I know that this sounds a little cryptic, and I know that it is leaving you wanting to scoot forward to the edge of your seat, but it's not cryptic, not at all. Everything I am going to share with you, at least in the front end, will simply be a history lesson of sorts, of which, all of you already know. Pastor Jimmy never even intended for anyone ever to read his journal, as I have already stated, but not because of any secrets he was holding. He was simply writing his thoughts down for his own benefit. That's it. That's all there is to that," and then Mark hesitated until he really had their undivided attention. "Except," Mark went on, "and here is where we come to it. Although he was not intentional about it, he was never the less faithful to record one small block of history, one inch at a time every week of his life. It's like reading an in depth accurate forty-year-long documentary that one might tune into once a week, and I got to read it after the fact all in just a few months. But this documentary was written by a dedicated follower of our Christ, using his faith and trust in God along with the Bible as his background. That, then, left me with an accurate history recording that included our Christian side of issues, unlike much of our current news media who broadcast their own interpretation of the life and times we live in.

"So, here's that epiphany. By reading the last forty years of a documented history recorded by a genuine follower of Jesus in just a few months was like watching the largest, longest hit on morality for all peoples, in fast motion. I got an upfront reminder of that last forty years of our political, national, social, economic, apathetic life styles, that have pushed the majority of all people, at least in America, further away from God and His teachings, and I got it all in just, what," and he looked to Martha for the time line but she just held up three fingers. "I guess it had to be three months and a couple of weeks of reading. It literally brought every one of those, *how could that be*, events close to my heart as if each one of them were happening for the first time right now, instead of over those forty years. But the sub-truth that existed, between the line also, that put a real kink in my, *how could that be*, mindset is the fact that along with the downfall of all peoples, was the downfall of much of our Christian communities, taking with them many of our Christian values. That, in your face, day to day reading of the last forty years, revealed all the elements of our demise, and why. But here again enters our human nature. Because all these events did take place over forty years the human in us had the tendency to dodge their importance, helping to magnify their outcomes because it was so long ago. More simply put, it's an out of sight out of mind pattern. And the further down that legendary Primrose Lane we wondered after the fact, the less important any of those elements became. In fact, that is the reason so many of those downfalls found success in the first place. And that is the reason we are taught to stay in touch with God, and with each other. You see when it, no matter what IT is, has gone on for so long, it gathers either positive, or negative momentum, and ceases to be able to be changed, stopped or corrected. Even the portrayal of positive and negative gets misconstrued, so that what really is positive becomes negative, and vice versa. So, since those brothers and sisters of ours, who are not following the teachings of Christ in so many areas of their lives, are susceptible to follow the teachings from anywhere else. That, in many cases, in many churches, is part of what has left our Christian communities fragmented and out of touch with each other. And like I said before, all of us do know the truth, and it's not that any of us don't know the history I have just named, but it's only by looking back on all that in such a short period of time, that I was able to see how destructive all of those wrong turns have been, what all the side effects are that have come from each one of them, and why it is so hard to do anything about any of it now.

"Reading Pastor Jimmy Lee Cambridge's journal allowed me to see truth written between the lines. Not only for what has happened, but what to do about it. And for sure, there actually is only one thing anyone can do about it. Martha gave it to me as an assignment to look for it. Reading those forty years of dedicated notes, forty years," he repeated and then paused, "in just over three months opened me up for what it was that I was supposed to find, and I found it."

"What is IT?" all of them spoke at the same time, and not in harmony. They all laughed briefly. "We ARE on the edges of our seats," Pastor Bleeker announced with a chuckle.

I'm Talking About Us Christians

"What IT is," Mark said, "requires a raft of identifiers. IT is what some Christian leaders and Christians have never stopped doing, although their numbers are shrinking. IT is what we always should have been doing and in truth have touched on sometimes, and IT is one of the most difficult easiest things we will ever have to re-think, re-evaluate, and re-build." Mark pauses again. "Please be patient with me as I repeat what I have already stated. IT is extremely easy, and IT is extremely difficult at the same time in each one of us. And US would include the majority of churches and Christian leaders as well. If WE want to first become a disciple of Jesus, and secondly want to successfully train up disciples who want to make disciples, WE need to make an about face. And finally, IT is right in front of us, easy to see, easy to know, easy to discover, but almost impossible for the majority of Christians to do…, and that is why we are having this discussion tonight."

Mark fell silent for a moment, and held up a finger to signal them to wait a moment. He turned around to fumble through his briefcase, and pulled out a stack of typed pages. "Here," he motioned to Randy, "pass these out, would you?" It was a single typed page, one side only. He waited until everyone had one, and then he continued. "That list could have been written by any one of you as well as myself, any time in the last couple of decades, or more maybe. That list of parasitic spiritual killers gives us a solid picture of most all the things that have anti-God written all over them, and there is nothing new there at all. There is nothing on that list that all of us don't already know all about." They all looked down at the page, and Mark fell silent again giving them all time to read the list, and even when he figured that they had to be finished, he waited for anyone to speak.

"Boy, that's some kind of list," Barbara was the first to speak up, "and you're right. As bad as all the things on this list are, there's nothing here that we all don't know about."

"Right," Mark confirmed quickly. "I agree, nothing new there at all, and every item on that list was found in Pastor Cambridge's journal, without even one of them being named, or specifically referred to. But each item on that list carried a heartbeat that strongly identified itself in not just one part only throughout his entire set of journals."

"All of us," Pastor Bleeker went on, "and most anyone else I know, within the Christian community that is, have

94

discussed every one of those items for years now, and we are very aware of how destructive each of them has been and are."

"And you are right yet once again," Mark said.

"So, what is it that you want us to do with this list, or should I ask what do you expect us to do about what's on this list?" Pastor followed with, "And please don't get me wrong. All of us are deeply concerned, but to date have been unable to curb even one of these issues."

"Again, you are as right as rain," Mark said, "there doesn't appear that any of us can do anything, as you say, to curb anything on that list. Well, except pray, and live our lives as an example. That does look like the only thing, realistically, we can do to help individuals see the light. We've tried hanging out banners, conducting outreach programs etc., and we have seen some fruit from all that. But generally speaking, many people, even some of our Christians, keep on marching to the beat of a different drum, don't they? No, reading that list really only amplifies the two quandaries that we have been and are in. We are unable to put our hand up to stop any of it, and secondly, we are on the wrong page anyway.

"Let me take you back to the first entry that Pastor Cambridge wrote that fired up my understanding." Mark looked down at his notes, "The entry was for June twenty-five, nineteen eighty-nine. That was the twenty-seventh anniversary, of the Supreme Court's ruling to remove sponsored prayer in all public schools in America. Reading that really disturbed me, because in nineteen eighty-nine, I, like everyone else I thought, agreed to that ruling. At that time, I had no clue that there was anyone, even those religious types, who could possibly object to that. They weren't being told not to pray, just not to pray in the public schools. Besides, I remember thinking, don't they have some kind of religious schools to go to? But, when I read Pastor Cambridge's notes about his sermon on that topic some twenty-seven years after the fact in his journal, my heart could easily see how destructive that one decision made by our Supreme Court had become. I could easily see how far reaching its outcome has been! How many important side issues, not immediately recognized to being connected, but eventually became kicked to the curb because of that one single act in history. But that wasn't all there was to it. I remember calling Martha for some additional input on that first discovery I made from his journal, to tell her that I thought that I had found what the pastor was hoping I would find, and she filled me into the rest of the story about that time back when he gave that sermon. In the end, and this is a really great example of what I am here for, I found out that since it had been twenty-seven years since that ruling had been irrevocably passed, most everyone didn't seem to be bothered by it any more. As a result of that sermon, Pastor did set up a time of prayer for our school systems, our government, and the Supreme Court, but after a couple of weeks, hardly anyone showed up to pray. And," Mark raised his voice in excitement, again gesturing with his arms above his head to amplify the thoughts of his heart, "I'm not talking about the general population of non-believers in our country not caring enough anymore about these kinds of issues, I'm talking about us Christians. That was only the start of my enlightenment. I kept reading his journal with my spiritual eyes open to seeing other such things that swayed our culture first, but also us Christians as well, from easy-to-understand truths, clearly identified in the Word of God. Why? I asked myself. What on earth could have done that? I also began to wonder how really far reaching all that had actually become. In essence, I was asking myself if it had become the problem, I thought I was seeing in our churches or was it just my imagination? Now to expel any fear that I might be wrong about my scrutiny, I know, and I'll share with you at another time if you like, that for certain I was and am not missing the mark here. If we, and I know all of you do, truly believe that the Bible is applicable for today's living in equal fashion as it was when Paul wrote it, then Ephesians six clearly identifies what is going on, who our enemy really is, and what we are supposed to do with it. On the whole, though, we don't often do, or don't do enough about any of the topics on that list. Although I do know of many well-informed Christians and churches who are on top of this battle field, there still remains a very high number of Christians who have lapsed into an apathetic view of "God is good, so I'm okay," type of mentality. That, then, helped me to understand why so many of us Christians, and again I am not referring only to our church, are living in doubt about what really is the truth on so many of those issues on that list, and why so many, easy-to-understand truths, sometimes, are not clearly identifiable by a higher number of Christians than one might believe.

"Let me follow up with this," Mark said. "There are diversions that have been used to keep our hearts and minds occupied, and thus unable or unwilling to become or stay on board with God's Word, and our Christian walk. Diversions that often times have been responsible for some Christians ending up in a stirred-up cauldron of what I call following the wrong shooting star. Those diversions can be anything that just isn't true at all, but looks so much like it is true to some, or even a group of individuals, that they buy into it hook line and sinker. That then becomes their focus on life, and following Jesus is a secondary venture. Or it could be something that really is partially true, so some easily take it to the next level and make it totally true. The end result is the same. That becomes the focus, and not Jesus, for their lives. Or, it could even be something that is a hundred percent factual, but it ends up being used as a club for others who are not doing what "I" think they ought to do. Or it is used as an excuse or the reason that they just don't follow the teachings of Christ all the way. I'm using the word diversions, but other descriptive words will work as well, like vain imaginations, or what is used in Proverbs, "our own understandings." But the point is that we have the capacity to pick up anything from anywhere and either choose to follow it out of the hand of God, or put it back into the hand of God. Examples aren't really needed here. All of you know of many such examples. Some of them have even been used to completely alter the meaning of God's Word, and some of them have often been used to refute God's Word. Basically, stating that "this" is right, and the Bible is not, and these ears of mine have heard from the mouths of people who made it clear that they truly believe that Jesus is the risen Son of God, and that

He died for their sins. Many, with some of the most distorted beliefs in some diversions to the truth, defend their lifestyle on every one of those issues I've listed there. "Yes," Mark said, pointing to two of the most common ones on the list he held up in front of him, "even those. And again," Mark said but then followed up with, "I know I have said this a lot, but it really needs to be understood. It is not only our wicked world around us that refuses to follow the teachings of Christ found in the Bible the way that it is. It is also some of our Christian family who have decided to follow a shooting star that leads slightly or completely away from Biblical teachings. Finally," he goes on to say, "one of the last of those diversions that have been used to be a most effective tool to place some of us in that cauldron, or to try to shut us Christians up and follow the leader down that Primrose Lane, is "Political Correctness." On the surface, that too sounds good, it makes sense, it is fair, it is accepted by many, and in and of itself is good. But the side effects that have come from that are devastating. I could go on, but like I said, the list on that page is not where we should be anyway. It's important to read this page, to understand what we can learn from that page, but, you see, it's our turn to do something about what's on that page. Something more than shyly turning our heads because we can't curb any one of those things," Mark concluded.

"When you said that we are on the wrong page anyway," Pastor Bleeker inserted, "referring to that list, I agree. But I think that you and all of us are on the same right page. Mark, it's so great to see how God moves when we get out of the way. You see, we chose to come here to this particular church. We prayed and felt that this church had what we were looking for in regards to making disciples who make disciples. That, in fact, was the biggest reason we wanted to be accepted here at this church, and why we finally accepted this commission."

"I can see that now," Mark said. But that list, like I have already stated, is and will be again, important to keep in front of us for a couple of really good reasons. Our goal, or let's say our charge, has never been a matter of morality in the first place. I am hitting heavily on that list, and even brought it to us tonight just to show you what I have discovered from those four journals, and how we can do something about it. Not the issues themselves, but for people in our church pews to regain a right standing with the Word of God. The lacking of godly morals has been evident from the day that Adam and Eve chose to disobey God. Our posture on immorality needs to be firm for sure, but only in reference to our own lives to be pleasing to our Lord, and to know what the Bible teaches us on any one moral issue so that we can teach it when called to do so. The reality is that we can't alter anyone's morality, and we shouldn't, and we are not called to do so." Mark held up one hand the same way a traffic policeman would to halt a line of oncoming cars. "Let me say that again because it is so important. We are not called to alter anyone's morality. We are called to alter our own, and that too is a key for us to be successful in making disciples. We aren't even called to show them, again whoever 'them' is, just how evil they are. Our

100

calling is so simple, so clear to understand, and additionally so not followed through with. That is why we are where we are, and not making disciples. THAT," Mark paused for effect again, "is what I have finally gotten out of Pastor Cambridge's journals."

They were an hour and a half into their hour-long meeting, so Pastor Bleeker suggested a break. As with any great meeting where great women are invited, great munchies are provided. They all got their coffee and cookies, and sat down to just converse on anything that came to mind. It was fascinating for Mark to listen in on some of their discussions where he discovered that just about everyone was talking about the journals, and what it may ultimately mean or do. That left Mark believing that he was on the right page after all.

But You
The Journal
7
Finale

Unless

After their break and everyone had found their seat again, Mark more or less picked up where he left off. "I was about to expound more on what I had finally gotten out of Pastor's journals, but first let me touch home on another truth. So far, we have been discussing, well for a lacking of a better way of putting it, all the ugly stuff around us, and in the church. So, to be fair," Mark said, "I want us to clearly recognize the other side of the coin. All of what I have just explained to you here tonight, is like telling the choir that they are all, every one of them, singing on a flat note, and that not even one of them could carry a tune in a plastic bag. The truth is that much of the choir is in tune, meaning those in all churches who truly follow the teaching of Christ, and the Bible, and there are many who genuinely and truly are. I know that too. If we were to make an in-depth investigation into that, we most likely would discover all the hundreds and thousands of generous, courageous, selfless, sharing, Spirit-filled, loving followers of our Lord, in prayer daily for the world we live in. But, please, just as surely as we are yet again discussing what we might be able to do to curb just some of this tsunami of evil that has taken so many of our Christian brothers and sisters hostage, let us come back to basics. First by recognizing that there is a problem, and then learn how *we* might proceed in discipling some of them back into a biblical stance of following Christ. Let's discover how we can perpetuate that process for the purpose of helping them make more disciples.

"Okay, I guess I have belabored that point long enough," Mark continued. "So, let's put that morality issue to bed. Let's try to identify what the problem really is, or if there is a problem that we could do anything about making disciples who make disciples. I hope that all of us can agree that that is our goal anyway? Truth be known, though, I believe my first goal needs to make sure that I am one of his true disciples. Desiring daily to do what Jesus taught. To take up my cross, deny myself, and follow Him."

"You can make that statement as an absolute desire of our hearts," Barbara said. "I can clearly see why we had to walk through a discussion on that morality vs immorality list. We need to understand that the list you made for us to look at isn't any kind of barrier for us, unless we let it. We can see the immorality around us, but we need to put their immorality into perspective, and remember that we too were just like that before we accepted Jesus as our Savior, *AND*," she strongly emphasized, "followed up with desiring to become His true disciple."

"That's the point," Mark said as he pointed a finger in her direction amplifying his agreement. "That is the truth, but that isn't really that clear for many Christians today to see. And that is because there are so many today who don't have a regular prayer life. Many don't read the Bible much anymore. Many come to church out of habit, or just to belong, or because they are trained to think that is what they are supposed to do to keep in tune with the rest of their congregation. Many, and I do mean many, will confirm that the only association with biblical teaching they have comes solely from their pastor's Sunday message. And many of them truly won't remember what that message was the day after, and I have discovered that their next connection with our Lord, or His Word won't be until next Sunday. That then has led any number of Christians into the lackadaisical life style we see, and that is the reason why over forty years so many have just fallen into a "whatever" way of thinking. That is also the reason why we clearly see people who say that they are believers, do just the opposite of what the Bible teaches to be correct because they just figure it out for themselves. "I can't see why..." What Pastor Cambridge's journal did for me, was to open my eyes to what, in spite of all that I have just played out as the problem, we *CAN* do about it."

"So, I think I know, but what can we do about it?" Pastor Bleeker asked.

"So," Mark comically mimicked his new pastor, "I will tell you what I came up with, and it is very basic. Let's call it Discipleship 101. We, meaning the whole of Christendom, have come up with program after program on how to follow through with Jesus' command to make disciples. All of those programs were, and are certainly well meaning, and most all of them have had some merit. Most all of them work some, but most all of them eventually just fade off into that, "well we tried," field of "what else can we do next?" dilemma. And, like I said, those programs are not all bad, but for the most part they really miss the mark. So, I ask, what should we do differently? Well, I am happy to announce that the answer to that question was written down for anyone to read and learn from in another journal penned a couple of thousand years ago. During my three plus months of reading Pastor Cambridge's journal, I learned how really easy it all is to go and make disciples of all nations. With that discovery, though, I also was reminded just how difficult it has always been to go and make disciples of all nations. That, then, was the major reason Pastor Cambridge gave me his journal. I tell you, God, and His Son Jesus, never made it difficult. We did, but before I go on, let me acknowledge the fact that many devoted, and sacrificial true believers have done it correctly for all the centuries, or we wouldn't be here at all. So, let's praise God for the faithful who came before us. We are having this meeting, solely to help set us back on the center line, like them, so as to be as effective as they were here in this place and in this time again.

"You see, when I finished reading all his journals my eyes were opened to what has happened to a large percentage of God's church. Pastor knew, as I do now, that it is critical for us to re-learn how to fight the good fight in a positive way, instead of working backwards from the issues we are facing. Like it or not, many times we are led by our fears in approaching the topic of how to make disciples. We don't need to figure it all out using some new or creative method of discipleship. Like I said, it's right in front of us. There are only a few simple steps each one of us needs to do to become ready to be truly successful in making disciples. Steps that, if genuinely followed, has to bring success in making disciples who in turn will make disciples. And success, among others, is a word whose idealistic view really needs some defining. But first let me remind you what those identifiers are that I mentioned before. IT is what we always should have been doing, but haven't been doing most of the time. IT is one of the most difficult easiest things we will ever have to re-think. IT is right in front of us, easy to see, easy to know, easy to discover, but almost impossible, with our present way of thinking, for the majority of Christians to do."

"Okay!" they all kind of announced at about the same time, "we are all ears," Randy spoke for the lot of them, "I think we know what some of those steps are."

"I'm sure you do, Randy. It's not a secret, and like I said, it's basic. But in that, knowing what our answers are, but not doing it is why it is so difficult. Not difficult for you, maybe, or me or many Christians, maybe, but because of our current apathetic society, it is definitely difficult to train other Christians to adopt… *UNLESS…*"

Mark pulled his two hands together palm to palm, and slowly slid them up in front of his face. He sat down with them, and, quietly began to speak. "You know, I started off this night with a disclaimer type of statement that basically said, that there was nothing in all of Pastor's writings, in and of itself, that would give us any insight as to what I am charged with to bring to you tonight. In addition, I told you all two other things as well. I said that all of this in the front end would simply be a history lesson, and secondly, that there was nothing here that you already didn't know. And, don't you know, all that is as true as chocolate is probably the world's most favorite candy. So…" Mark said raising his hands in the air as if giving up, "the difference now, vs. any other time in our church's history, or on any corner of the world for that matter in any church that names Jesus as Lord is that we are seeing a continuous drain on a large percentage of Christian's lives. Many are walking willingly, although ignorantly, into our enemy's line of fire, and not being trained to fight back. In many instances, they don't even realize that they are under fire. It has always been important for us to combat evil, and to understand how we are to combat evil, but we are seeing so many Christians falling helplessly short of being able to take up the sword of the Spirit. Now the war between good and evil has been raging since Adam and Eve, as I have already alluded to. It's because of that, *'impossible to win war,'* that God our Father, out of incalculable love, sent His only Son Jesus into the world, with absolutely no requirements for us at all, except to simply believe in His Son as Savior of our lives for eternity. Now, it was God the Father's only Son Jesus who brought to us the great commission to go and make disciples. That should be easy enough for any beginning believer in Jesus to understand what needs to be done. The problem doesn't start there, though. It starts sometime after that when they are not given the opportunity, or they decide that they don't want or need to be trained further than just believing in Jesus. And like I said, there are so many aids in our current society to drag them out of the classroom where God's teachers are, and into a field of dreams loaded with all their friends. So, the question *why is that*, still rakes our conscious thoughts, doesn't it? The list of steps that I have put together is designed to help us overcome that "why" question. That list is created to help ME first, not any of them. Not anyone else but me. For me to capture *my* humility, *my* memory, *my* ideals, *my* imaginations, *my* vision of what *my* mission is, *my* work I am doing for the Lord. In addition, it is designed to capture anything else in me that would set itself up against any and everything God would want me to think, be, act, or to do. And then to bring all of those things captive to Him and His Holy Spirit. Thus, helping me to get back to basics to be HIS disciple, being content in all things from then on.

"Jesus, when he walked the earth with his disciples, didn't tell them to pay attention because there might be a quiz at the end," Mark continued. "They, at least at first, didn't even know there would be an end. He just walked with them knowing that eventually they would "get it." That was how He

108

discipled them, after He chose them and told them to "follow me, and I will *MAKE* you fishers of men." Jesus' instruction was first of all "believe." Secondly to go and help others believe. It was not given to them to make disciples until Jesus' ascended into heaven. But it was then that He said to them all, "Teach them to observe all things that I have commanded you." He also told them that, "All authority has been given to Me in heaven and on earth. GO therefore and make disciples of all the nations." If any believer can grasp that, he or she will understand that His authority as far as making disciples has been given to us, his sheep. Authority implies responsibility, but the truth is that the responsibility command came from the words "GO," and "TEACH THEM." So often what we have done, inadvertently, has been to apply pressure to our team mates, meaning those who are followers of Christ, by instructing them of their responsibility. That then, in many cases, has left them feeling guilty if they wouldn't or couldn't succeed. And there's that word succeed again. We really need to discuss what success is," Mark injected. "But sometimes we have made it sound like they are lower on the food chain of those who are pleasing to God. What we have missed so often is how to teach our disciples, and even ourselves, who are to make disciples about God's authority that has been given to each true believer in Christ. That is a gift God gave us so that we have the ability to succeed. Sometimes, and I will say again that it may be well intended, but we are attempting to train new disciples how they are to act, what they are supposed to say, what they are supposed to do, to be etc. Now, all that does need to be taught, but that all will come out in perfect unison when you have in your midst a genuine seeker desiring to follow the Christ who pulled them up out of the miry clay."

Mark added, "These steps, I am talking about, are what each of us needs to do individually. Additionally, *when* you are given a seeker to mentor, those steps are the very first things you need to teach to them, just after you ascertain that he/she is a genuine believer who will confess that Jesus is the risen Son of God and that He died for my sins.

"So," Mark stood up again, "let me conclude tonight with this. These steps I wrote and will give to you, again I say, are just for you, for me, or for any individual to follow through with, or not. You will certainly be able to identify each step on that list, but I want to encourage you to read each one of them and to follow through with what it is asking you to do. It has to be that you really want to do this. I can only promise you that if you truly, from your heart choose to follow through with this set of steps, and do it continuously, you will see a change in your own life, and you will see how making disciples isn't difficult at all. What you, me, or anyone else who truly wants to be an effective part of going out and making disciples, needs to recognize is that it is me, not them, who has to humble myself before the Creator of all things *afresh*, *anew*, and *again*, and *again, daily,* so that I can be judged by Him, not anyone else, to be one of His true disciples. That then, being the first of six total steps, will enable you, or me, or whoever follows through, to be led by God's Holy Spirit, for God's glory, to move onto the next steps."

Mark turned and fumbled again through his briefcase. "Here" he asked Randy again, "would you pass these out? This is the whole list of steps I have typed out for us. This is only the beginning of IT being one of the most difficult easiest things to do. And again, I will tell you that the difficult part of all these steps is to simply follow through with doing it. Not one step that I have listed there will be difficult to achieve, if you choose to do them. We can't allow IT to end here. We, each one of us, needs to take those simple, but vital steps to heart and pray daily for our own personal involvement, but also for each of the rest of us."

Mark looked at Pastor Bleeker, "That's about all I have to share tonight, but I would strongly ask that we all get together at some time in the future after we have completed all those steps."

"I'll put together some times when we might have a second meeting, and let you all know," Pastor Bleeker announced.

"Actually," Mark countered, "maybe it would be best if everyone took a long look at the list tomorrow, and then we can talk about setting up another meeting. I think there is enough to consider there on that list to keep us all busy for a while." At that, Mark fell silent turning around again to put his briefcase in order and closed the lid and latched it.

Pastor Bleeker stood, "I know this lasted quite a bit longer than planned, but it was worth it. Thanks, Mark, for your faithfulness. Let me close in prayer."

When they had all left the church, Mark found himself standing outside with Martha. He had walked her to her car and in her own quiet kind of relief, she said, "Mark, you did good, Jimmy would have been proud."

"Pride," Mark grimaced, "doesn't that come right before the fall?"

Martha reached up and gently placed her hand on Mark's shoulder. "You know what I mean. Certainly I, with you, give all glory to God for any outcome after tonight. I think your list of steps is going to be a real stepping stone to get all of us back into the, what should I call it, a discipleship M.O."

"Oh, Martha, that's pretty good, modus operandi. I like that. Our new mode of operation. But you know that that list of steps is designed uniquely for one person. That being me, or you, or for the one reading the list of steps. From that, hopefully, we will connect so that it becomes a *we* thing."

"It's too late for me to get into your list tonight, but I will first thing in the morning." Martha said with a wave of her hand turning toward her car.

"But," Mark followed up with, "let's continue to pray that we will all be ready when we start receiving people to mentor."

She turned around again to face Mark, "Well, that's a positive sense of," and she stopped talking, looked up at Mark with a grin on her face and continued, "IT is going to happen!"

"Martha," Mark said with an equally distinctive grin on his face. "You certainly are a jewel."

"That's okay, Mark," she said as she turned to get into her car. "Good bye, and you have a good night."

"Bye," Mark said, and in his usual way, he just waved his hand over his shoulder as he walked to his car. It has been a very long haul, he thought as he climbed in behind the steering wheel. He started the engine and stretched leaning back in his seat for one brief moment, and then he put the car in gear and headed home looking to own a deserved peaceful night's sleep.

But You
The Journal
8
Changing of the Guard

Oh, you devil

Mark's drive home was a very thoughtful time. He tossed words, ideas and ideals that had been spoken of in his meeting with the pastor and the elders back and forth in his mind. He tried to imagine what they thought, what they might do, or not do. He also tried to imagine what it would look like if we all climbed on board with what he was seeing as a fresh start in their church for developing disciples. He played with those thoughts, like a kindergartener in a sandbox full of too many toys to choose from. He was exhausted when he got home, so he just plopped down in his recliner, and prayed. *"What just happened Lord? Did they listen? Did I do any good at all? Did I make a mountain out of a mole hill about Pastor Cambridge's journal?"* and for maybe one minute, no more, Mark found himself in a state of mind, much like he imagined

Elijah would have been in after he was used so impressively by God for the children of Israel by calling fire down from heaven, but then fearing for his life and running away. But suddenly, "Mark," he mouthed through clenched teeth, "you don't even listen to yourself, do you?" He leaned forward in his chair, and burst out laughing. "Oh, you devil," he bellowed to the silent room that surrounded him, "you are tricky, aren't you?" He stood up and waved his hand at nothing in particular, "You have no place here. Get out of my life, my house, and my mind, in Jesus' name!" Mark commanded. "Oh, how easy am I anyway?" he confessed through a winning grin on his face. "Thank you, Lord, and help me to keep my guard up better next time." Mark packed up all his cares, pushing them all the way to the bottom of his *"I don't need to worry about this imaginary box of tricks,"* and went to bed. He did, in fact, have a deserved peaceful night's sleep.

The next morning, he got up refreshed and went to work. When he got home that afternoon he went straight to his desk, turned his computer on, and opened the file he had created days before labeled *"Steps for a Renewed Heart for Discipleship."* He read the first couple points, and leaned back in his chair. Mark momentarily became conscious that he was talking to himself again, but didn't care. "This will work, and once again I see how really simple it all is. Wow! I hope everyone can see its importance, and how easy it is. The only difficult thing about any of this the same thing that has always made it difficult, but even that is easy to see, believe and to understand, if one has a desire to do so. It all comes down to believing that this is what You want, Lord, and then," he held his thought, got up and walked into his living room. In moments his recliner found him. "I remember having this conversation with Pastor Jimmy once, a long time ago, and again with myself just after I finished complaining about that other church," he said as he sat down. "I was so frustrated, and what was it I said? Oh yeah, I remember. It takes dedicated discipline, that's what I said it takes."

Mark just fell silent diving into his "recall" state of mind, reliving that entire conversation he conducted with himself several weeks prior. He remembered questioning... "So, what is keeping us Christians frozen to our *'I'll just let someone else do it, box of excuses'?* Is it laziness? Or maybe it's just that it requires some effort that seems to be so far out of the norm for them that they just don't feel the need to bother? Boy I think that has to be part of it. I know that one major thing is that in order to really put yourself totally into this, you have to," and Mark remembered chuckling at his own analogy. "Yeah, that is the key, isn't it? In order to put yourself totally into this," and he chuckled again, "all you have to do is put yourself totally into this," and he smiled now at the thought he had then. He almost had a photographic memory of this let's-work-it-out discussion that he had just weeks before, and he continued. "That brings us back to not being able to serve two masters, doesn't it? The more we are wrapped around our personal, political, and social goals, the less we are interested in putting ourselves totally into following all the teachings of Christ, instead of leaning heavily, or only, on His mercy, love and forgiveness. Wow," Mark thought, "that is an interesting nest of what is going on, isn't it?" He remembered what his next thoughts were… "What that has done, has created an easy way out for not becoming His active disciple. Of course, that, then, leaves us crippled to be able to teach anyone else, like our kids, our grandkids or anyone else who is watching us Christians to see if there is any difference between what they believe and what we believe. Boy," Mark mouthed the word silently, remembering speaking them out loud then, "that is the problem, and therein lies much of the reason for many of our Christian's lacking." Apathy, was his next thought, he remembered, to be the word he keeps coming back to. "We are so wrapped up in a 'whatever' attitude, that we either don't think about the calling on our lives, or we just don't take it seriously. And, of course, that then, after a long enough period of time living with that as their day-to-day format of spirituality, it's easy to become imbedded deeper and deeper into thinking that that is just fine with God, and the circle is complete. The end result is what we are facing on a regular basis in so many churches. But then from that stems all the excuses I have ever heard, from *"It's the pastor's job, that's why we pay him,"* to *"That's not my calling, doesn't God have people to do that sort of thing?"* along with a multitude of really good sounding and seemingly easily understood excuses that just make sense to them. Either way, from all of that, we are facing a second situation that puts another crimp in our disciple making efforts, and that is the burden that has surfaced on some of our church leaders, that is bringing many of them to just give in or give up.

"Boy," Mark said out loud again, "If I had recorded those thoughts I had back then, I'll bet I could play it back now, and it would be identical to the thoughts I am having now."

Mark got up out of his recliner and returned to his desk. He closed his file on "Steps," and opened another file he had made about this topic a while back titled, *"Reasons Why a Christian Isn't Discipled."* Mark just stared at the list on his computer. After some thought, he said, "I am not finding fault with them really, I am praying for them, because they are part of us. They're true believers who have accepted the truth that Jesus died for their sins. They are our brothers and sisters. They are part of God's kingdom *AND*," Mark concluded, "they, like so many over the centuries, have simply been deceived into thinking that since they have God's grace, and that His mercies are new every morning, that they don't need to do anything else. What really keeps them deceived, though about becoming an active disciple wanting to make a disciple, is that most of them are really good people. They try to live their lives doing and being *good*, and that again comes back to them judging themselves as *moral*, so they are *okay* with God. Wow," Mark said, "but what they need is mentored and discipled. That is all they need, and that needs to be our first target market." He remembered back to when he wrote this list he was looking at again, and what he thought then. "I have known that for a long time now. The question has always been what can we do to help those in our church pews who seem to be totally content with just receiving from God a sermon each Sunday, and stopping right there? Or the ones who only go to church when they feel like it or on holidays? How do we get them up and out of our sanctuary doors to be discipled in the first place, so that they will have the confidence to want to disciple someone else?" Mark remembered giving a nod of approval to each entry on the list. The list was long, and there weren't any titles on the list that didn't also provide sub notes under each topic. He began to read the list out loud, and right at the top of the list was the word in caps and bolded...

- **APATHY!!**
  Indifference, Lethargy, Laziness, Boredom, Ennui,

Also, on his list, he had made additional notes for each of the sub notes, and he now remembered that under the word ennui, which he had never heard of before, he noted the words *"world-weariness."* He found that when he looked it up. He went on reading, but noticed that over half of his entire page fell under that main listing...APATHY. Mark stopped reading, and figured that just about every reason or excuse for a true believer not following through with Jesus' command to GO make disciples, and TEACH them to obey all that I have taught you... was a condition that could easily fall under that one header, "apathy."

Mark continued to read his list.

- **Entitlement**

  The belief that one doesn't need to earn something, all you need to do is just get it, and in some cases, it doesn't matter how. It almost falls in the thought that *"God did it, I got it, so that's the end of that."*

- **Desensitizing**

  Remember the frog story. A live frog sits in a pan of water on the stove. The burner is lit, but the temperature of the water increases so slowly that the frog doesn't notice that it is getting hot enough to cook him.

- **Not believing**

  That "I" can be used by God

  Feelings of inferiority, or lack of being encouraged

  No one was available to mentor or disciple

  Unwillingness to get deeper involved

"Now that subtitle can cover a lot of ground," Mark remembered thinking... "That can come from any number of situations, some as simple as not knowing what to do exactly. Or maybe the common thinking that basically says, *"why would God use me?"* Or, just not understanding how much God does not have any favorites, not believing that God would and has used small children, and disabled people, and the least of these, for His purpose and His glory. Maybe not believing that one can be used by God is a result of misinformation, followed up with no one able or willing to give correct answers to unasked questions. Or, it could be a simple matter of someone feeding misinformation, because they themselves were deceived. That could even happen," Mark thought, "from seriously well-meaning, but totally out of bounds relatives or friends."

"Mark," he said out loud. "You went through this exact analogy already. What possible good can come from this?" but he kept on reading.

- **Lack of knowledge**
  Almost the same as above, and carrying the same result.
- **Embarrassment**
  Being taken out of our comfort zone.
  Family settings where some, or the majority has made it clear that they are not believers, and one then is forced to make a choice to stand up for their faith, or just let it slide.
  Courage vs humiliation, awkwardness, or just unsure
- **Lack of the desire**
  to be known for what "I" truly believe
- **Following the wrong star**
  particular church-enforced doctrine, denominational edicts, traditions, or personal ideals
  Legalism
  Learning to be obedient on the LAW of God's Word only. Obeying only the "do's and don'ts taught from a leadership positioning, or traditions, or from your own ideals
  Freedom in Christ to the point that He did it all, so I don't have to do anything

- **Ignoring**

  what you are being taught that is correct from the Bible, and accepting first what your mother, your father, your older esteemed brother or what you think your priest or pastor has always taught you
- **Growing up in some major distress**

  No real role models

  Being abused in a variety of ways, leaving one unable to trust anyone for anything

"That list was very long," Mark said, "way too long." He remembered making the list in an attempt, not to find fault, but to be better prepared to minister to someone who might come up with one of those statements. Mark stopped reading. But all that doesn't matter anyway, does it Mark?" he said to himself again. "In fact," he continued, "that list of why Christians from all eras don't, won't or can't be fully indoctrinated into becoming a disciple of Jesus has always been. Furthermore, if the list of why's were complete, there wouldn't be enough paper and ink to handle them all. No, the important thing for me, or for any Christian who really wants to be known for being a disciple of Christ to remember, is not about why they are not becoming one of Jesus true disciples, nor does it have anything to do with them not doing something correctly, or what they are doing that is headed in a misguided direction. In fact, it has nothing to do with them at all. What the only important thing for me to know is what am "I" doing about becoming one of Jesus's real disciples myself, so that God can use me for his purpose and His glory, and to be fully prepared to address any one of those why's, when I am called to do so."

Mark, in one quiet quick flip of his wrist, deleted that entire file from his computer. "There is nothing there that I want to remember," he said, and he reopened the other list he had given to the group the night before: *"Steps for a Renewed Heart for Discipleship."* "Now this is where all of us need to start. Not on what THEY are, or are not. Not on what THEY do or do not, but on ME and what I am or am not, and on ME and what I do or not do." And again, he said, "It needs to start right here with **me**." Mark began to read the pages that he had printed and handed out to his church leaders the night before. There was a short note he had written prior to his list of steps. "Starting tomorrow morning before I go to work," Mark thought, "this is going to be my daily exercise."

Dear Pastor, Elders, and ladies:

It is up to you individually if you care to follow through with this list, but like I have already mentioned, a good rule here would be that if you do choose to walk through it, do it with all your heart.

Steps for a Renewed Heart for Discipleship
1. <u>**Recognition**</u>

It is me, not anyone else I may have ever considered, who is in need of humbling before God afresh daily, so that I can be used by HIM whenever, however HE wants...Then be *thankful* every day, *trusting* in Him every day, and giving Him *glory* every day. Start each day early, by acknowledging who He is, and who you are not. Pray and meditate on this truth. Take some time on this. Don't be too quick to just finish this step. Make it count. Ask God to help you become a prayer warrior for Him, to become His ambassador and a minister of His Word.

2. **Get Real**

   I know that you know this, **but** it is time to *get real* about who your enemy is, and what he is about, and what he wants to do, and, - **IF YOU LET** him, what he can do to you. *1 Peter 5:8 "Be sober, be vigilant; because your adversary the devil walks about like a roaring lion, seeking whom he may devour."* Key into these words: Be vigilant, walks around, roaring lion, seeking someone to DEVOUR. That someone can be you, and he isn't kind at all. He wants to kill. I know that you know this also, **but** it is time to *get real* about who you are in Christ. *1 John 4:4 "You are from God, little children, and have overcome them, because He who is in you is greater than he who is in the world."* Key into these words: You are from God, have overcome, and greater than. And that last word needs to be said again and again. GREATER is He who is in you.

And finally, you need to know that everything in these first two steps is for you to start to renew your heart for discipleship. Take your time each day completing this step over, with as much heart as the first day you started doing this.

Here is where some changes can take place, IN ME. I know that you have heard those Scriptures before. I know that you have understood those Scriptures for years. But it is the "I know," that has in part gotten many of us backed into a corner without realizing it. These first couple of steps are designed simply to put us back on track with an acute awareness anew of who we are, who we are not, who HE is, and who we are not, and why we have difficulty with anything, let alone knowing how to reach people to disciple them. Reread those Scriptures every day, no matter how repetitive it becomes, for one week. Additionally, each day you read them, read it as if it is the first time you are reading it. Slow down to make it fresh, and it's better if you start your day with this instead of finishing your day with this. But just those couple of passages are not enough. To complete this assignment correctly, read also 1 Peter 5: 1-11 and the whole chapter of 1 John 4. Take some time after to pray and to contemplate on all those Scriptures. Get real about their authenticity. Finally, start to pray, maybe like you already have from time to time, but every day asking God's Holy Spirit to speak to you like never before. Ask God that if there is

ANYTHING in you that is, even innocently in the way of you getting closer to HIM, to show that to you.

IMPORTANT...Don't go on to step three until you have done these first two steps faithfully for a week. Trust me on this. I know that you already know all this. I know that this is basic, but it's like building a wall that will serve as a blockade against our preconceived standards and our enemy. At the same time that wall will once again become a renewed start to form in ME, a firm and solid foundation.

3. **Take a Stand**

Make sure that anyone, maybe everyone you know, KNOWS beyond any doubt who you are in Christ. Go out of your way to announce deliberately to all what you believe and who you believe in. Make it an absolute that you believe the Bible is the Word of God. If challenged about some topic in the Bible you are not sure about, or you are totally lost on, simply confess honestly the truth. You can say something like, *"you know, I'm not sure. In fact, there are many things that I yet don't understand, but that does not make it wrong, it only means that I am still learning."* BUT, above all...don't be shy. If you truly believe that Jesus IS the Christ of God...MAKE IT KNOWN. Again, I say though, be proactive about being known. Go out of your way to let everyone you work with, you play golf with, you have any connection with, know where you stand and why. Don't make it a simple side statement either. SAY IT plainly. *"This is who and what I am."*

This step three is probably the most important step you will ever make toward being prepared to be one of Jesus' disciples. As you look over that step again, you may be one who has made the assumption that everyone you know already knows that. That you have been a solid church goer for decades and it's just taken for granted that they know. Don't you believe that *"get out of jail free card,"* you've just made for yourself for a second. Go out of your way and tell them, even if they know. And remember that even when you do go out of your way to tell them, and they say that they already know that you are, three main issues are automatically being covered. The first is that even though they say they knew, they are now in the position to wonder why you had to say it, and will take you very seriously on your faith from now on. Secondly it is a high possibility that even though they knew that about you, that one or more of them have need to talk to someone about their own faith, and guess who that someone is likely to be? And thirdly, it will eliminate the temptation for you to inadvertently slide into one of their "out of bounds" side games, however innocent it may appear. Be prepared, though, in any case to be silently disavowed by some groups once you do that. Count that all joy though.

After you have taken step three, go back and continue to do steps one and two, and review step three praying if there is anyone else you can tell. Give yourself extra days, or even another week just to make sure you have told everyone in your family and friends who Jesus is in you, continuing to read those first Scriptures along with your normal daily devotions.

4. **Correct**

Go back in your memory, asking God to reveal to you anyone, or anything, that you have done that needs to be brought to the surface. Something that you need to repent from. Something that you did to someone, however small, that you need to set right. Something you know that you didn't handle like you were supposed to as a Christian. Go to him/her/or them and correct. Apologize where appropriate, make amends where appropriate, confess your error, making sure that they understand that you also erred against God, and that is the reason you felt it important to make this correction. Even in the event that you know that you were not the one who was at fault, and that you didn't do anything that requires correction, go and try to make them understand that you would like to be part of making things right between you and them. Obviously though, if you are not guilty of anything there is no need to apologize, but this exercise will free you from wondering what to do next, if they think you are guilty.

Step four is very interesting and can end up becoming a burden that you don't need to have, so let's take a closer look at this. The word that comes to mind is wisdom. All through the book of Proverbs we read about wisdom, so let me share some here with you. Certainly, you have confessed all your sins to God, and because of His promise, you are forgiven. Now, before we go on in this step, go back to step two. Remember who you are in Christ, and remember who your enemy is, and what he wants to do. When you begin to take step four to heart, be wise in your next move. Get some advice from another sister or brother in Christ if you need to about any specific situation you feel you need to correct. If you have been bothered by something for a long time. Something, maybe you did, or should have done, and a negative outcome came from it and you blame yourself. No matter how big or small the issue is, or was doesn't matter. And if know you can't do anything about it now, you need to do what we all have had to do with any situation like that. And I know it's easier said than done, but all you can, and need to do, is simply forgive yourself and go on. The second bit of wisdom is that you will be stuck behind one of our enemy's eight balls if you don't. And this is the reason for step four. When we teach someone else the importance of forgiveness, don't we sometimes forget, or maybe the word to use is fail, to forgive ourselves? This is how that goes sometimes, *"God has forgiven me, I know, but look what I have done. It's so bad, I just can't forget it."* For you to become a teacher of disciples, you need to cross that bridge. You simply need to forgive yourself in the same way your heavenly Father has already forgiven you. That's it! Don't let it fester in you anymore! God sent His only Son, Jesus, for that purpose alone.

And it's not just for them...it's for you. For you to continue to hang onto that will only allow your enemy to continue to convince you that you really can't be Jesus' disciple. Don't let him have his way with you any longer.

Remember also that this step four is an ongoing issue, so give yourself grace. You may, and should, find it more prudent to just let something you have done be forgotten, receiving God's grace for you and His forgiveness, and NOT trying to make any correction for it. There is wisdom too, in that, if in trying to make corrections that will ease your conscience you hurt the other party. Be wise.

As you conduct step four, which may take a while, don't lose track of the first three steps. Daily continue to go over them, and pray. Naturally pray for all the things you are habited in praying for, but make your fist prayer, and it's not selfish, for yourself. The reason it isn't selfish is because what you are in essence praying for yourself is that you are becoming a teacher of disciples. And that leads me to step five.

5. **The Beatitudes**

This step will require you to add to your daily reading. Read Matthew 5: 1-20. It's not just the "Blessed are," verses, but additional information that Jesus is giving to us all. This may be the start for you to reassociate yourself on what it means to be a disciple of Jesus. Again, remember that although this is basic in our already knowledgeable minds, it still remains one of the best disciplines we can do.

Keep up with steps one, two, three, and four as you read and reread this section of Matthew daily for no less than one additional week. By this time, you should be into week four or five. What you are doing here is basically re-indoctrinating yourself away from any fault finding, away from seeing what is wrong or right with anyone, or anything, including the world around you, and re-fitting yourself to concentrate only on "my" stance with God's Holy Spirit, so that Christ can be glorified if He chooses to use me. We can't be ignorant of the world around us, but if we let it, we can be pulled into believing that we have to do something about it. At this juncture, you only need to gain access to God's holy power, and that only comes through your submission to Him. This is a way to do that. You are changing your goals from you being right, to seeing Him be right.

6. **Fruit of the Spirit**

This step truly hits us sincerely between the eyes compared to the more accepted ideals of the world around us. BUT, brother or sister in Christ, we need to examine ourselves and although we are living in this age of Grace because of Jesus, we nevertheless need to add step six to our daily reading.

Galatians 5: 14, *"For all the law is fulfilled in one word, even in this: "You shall love your neighbor as yourself."*

Galatians 5: 17, *"For the flesh lusts against the Spirit and the Spirit against the flesh; and these are contrary to one another, so that you do not do the things that you wish."*

Galatians 5: 19-21, *"Now the works of the flesh are evident, which are: adultery, fornication, uncleanness, lewdness, idolatry, sorcery, hatred, contentions, jealousies, outbursts of wrath, selfish ambitions, dissensions, heresies, envy, murders, drunkenness, revelries, and the like; of which I tell you beforehand, just as I also told you in time past, that those who practice such things will not inherit the kingdom of God."*

Galatians 5: 22-23, *"But the fruit of the Spirit is love, joy, peace, longsuffering, kindness, goodness, faithfulness, gentleness, self-control; against such there is no law."*

The very first assignment on this step is to memorize each of the nine fruits of the Spirit, found in verses 22-23.

Then every morning, maybe while you are having your morning coffee, read Galatians 5 and look to see yourself in these verses, whether for the good or bad. This will aid you to become better and better at identifying the fruit of the Spirit that you most need help with. Pray, then, asking God to help you produce that fruit.

All the steps I have put on my list are critical. And all of these steps are easy to conduct and conclude. This last step is just as simple, but I think this step brings an understanding of exactly where I am, compared to where I should be according to what God's Word shows me.

Add this as your daily reading. I know that reading this much every day may become a small burden, but I encourage you to do this. If you do this faithfully for one more week, all of these steps together will start to transform your heart's interest. You will be brought into the presence of God, for some maybe, like never before. It's here where we should start to experience what one of our favorite song's lyrics give us about the things of this world growing dimmer, in the light of His glory.

Let me encourage you once again on this topic. Doing this, reading all this, will take maybe an extra thirty minutes each day, depending on how much time it takes you to read and pray. But please, take whatever time you need to do this with a heart of worship, praise, and a prayer asking God to SHOW ME, whatever. What we all need to do is bypass the temptation to simply believe that all these Scriptures are so basic. That we have all seen, read, and even taught from them for a long time, so we don't need to give them all the thought that I am asking you to give. Rather, we need to dive into them anew, on a daily basis, to allow God's Holy Spirit to heal us of anything. To fill us fresh, and bring each of us back into the center of His will to become not only His skilled teacher of future disciples, but most importantly, that we are in tune with His will, and that our hearts are once again on fire for what He wants, without worrying about any outcome.

When all of us who wish to have completed all these steps, let's get together and just round table type talk about it all. This should be in about five to six weeks.

Mark Garner

Mark looked up at the clock when he finished reading, and noted that he had been at this from the time he got home from work for a couple of hours. He was hungry, so he closed up his computer and ventured into his kitchen hoping to find something easy to make for his dinner, but he wasn't successful. He didn't have any left overs, and after rummaging through his fridge and cupboards, he couldn't find one idea that would satisfy, so he decided to just give it up and call Martha.

"Martha, its Mark. Just called to see if you had had a chance to peruse the list, I gave everyone?" There was a long silence that followed, and Mark said out loud, "oops."

"No, Mark, don't jump to conclusions. It is fantastic. I only paused to answer because the steps are so full of truth. I've been a pastor's wife for over forty years. I know the Bible pretty much inside out, figuratively speaking, but this is such an eye opener. And you are right, it is simply basic."

"Well," Mark commented, "don't think that I am so smart. What you are reading in those steps is what I need to start doing as well. It's not just "them," again whoever "them" is, who needs to have a genuine alignment, it's me too. But I do honestly believe that by doing this, it will alter my outlook on everything, including my City Outreach. I'm going to

134

propose that all our companions in that outreach get a copy of that list as well."

"There were a couple of items I think should be added to your list, though," Martha said. "I do think that you covered them, but it may be important to make them a bit stronger."

"Shoot," Mark said, "I absolutely trust your input."

"Just four items. You definitely touched on forgiveness in your one step you named "Correct," and you hit on unforgiveness of ourselves. But I was thinking that I have witnessed some people who have had some really awful things happen to them, that they have difficulty forgiving. That's huge in their walk with the Lord. Usually that is one area where that person just gets stuck, well like you said behind one our enemy's eight balls."

"You are correct, and thank you for that reminder. That is one of the most difficult areas to minister to also. I remember a few cases like that. If we meet someone with that unfortunate problem, we will minister to them separately, before we take them through these six steps. They can't go on anyway until they have forgiven that person, persons, or events that wounded them so deeply. Don't forget also that that same unforgiveness needs to be addressed for people who can't or won't forgive something that really never existed, but think it has. That takes a great deal of patience. That will take some extra love and care. We can bring that up, well actually, periodically during our ongoing meetings. Either as a general teaching, or on a specific discipleship case. What are the other three?"

"Again," Martha went on, "you touched on laying down all malice, anger, and hatred. All that sometimes falls under unforgiveness as well. I just wanted to bring them to the surface again, maybe to enlighten the reader of your steps to be aware of how destructive carrying that around can be to themselves. We do patiently, caringly understand the hurts that brought that about in their lives, but at the same time, since they have admitted to accepting Jesus, they need help with that so that they can move on. Even sometimes some of them are living with that malice unaware of what exactly happened to them, but still, they need some kindness, and some prayer and some real ministering to. The only way any one can rid themselves of malice is by giving it to the Lord in prayer, and coming to one of us to walk along with them through the whole process. The other two items that I was thinking about are pride and arrogance. But that is what you are attempting to do with your steps, isn't it? Those steps are going to be used by any one of us who really grasps the importance of coming back to those basics of becoming a true disciple of Christ, so that we will be totally prepared to step up to the plate, willingly, joyfully, and go out of our way to minister to anyone who needs us."

"That's exactly what I am attempting to do, well, in my life first, but yes to help anyone else who knows that this is a very good method of being discipled, and will be the tool to set us up to be prepared to disciple anyone we, or someone else, leads to Jesus."

"Mark," Martha spoke in a soft kind voice, "I miss my Jimmy, and I know you do as well, but isn't it a thrill to see that because of his journaling all those years, fruit is coming directly from Jimmy's work?"

"It is," Mark agreed, "and an additional blessing that I have received from these last few months of going through his journals was that it often made me feel like he was right here going through it with me."

"What's your next move in regards to your list of *"follow me as I follow Christ,"* steps you wrote out for us? Or, should I say how are you going to dig a trench for our new discipleship M.O?" Martha asked.

"You really do have a vivid way of laying everything out, don't you? My next step is to wait until next week after Pastor's sermon on Sunday. I'll give him a call and see what he thinks about the list. You know me, Martha, I will follow his lead. As I said, I am going to go through and complete this exercise to the full extent, but whatever he wants to do for the church is up to him. I am a firm believer that he is my new spiritual leader on this earth, and that it was God who put him in that position over me. Pastor Jimmy taught me that. After that we'll see what Pastor Bleeker wants to do."

"You take care of yourself Mark, and I'll see you in church on Sunday."

"You as well, Martha Cambridge, see you then and there," and, "bye," was all she got, and he just waved his hand over his head like he always did when he hung up the phone.

It was Friday night, and Mark had nothing to do. He had faithfully completed his assignment with all of Pastor Cambridge's journals, was content that his list of steps to renew his heart for discipleship really was, not only the next best step for himself, but the _only_ next best step for himself. He sat down in his recliner again thinking, hoping, praying that it wouldn't stop with only him to complete. He did feel somewhat relieved that he was finished with the journals, but also experienced a mild let down as he didn't have anything to do in its place. It was getting late, but he didn't have to work the following day, so he wasn't worried about getting to sleep early. He decided to go out to get something to eat. He looked up at the clock again. It was just past eight o'clock. He grabbed his jacket and keys, opened his front door, locked it behind him, and "Steak, how about a steak Marcus old boy? You need to have steak."

Mark didn't put any more effort into thinking about the _journal syndrome_, as he was starting to call it. He had made up his mind that he had done everything he was supposed to do, and even felt totally content with the idea that even if no one else ever found value in his list of steps, that he knew he already had.

But You

The Journal

9

Outcome

Grouping of ME's

Pastor Bleeker's sermon on Sunday morning was, "Boy that's timely," Mark thought, <u>on discipleship</u>. What really impressed him was that there must have been half a dozen times in his sermon where he made comment about… "getting back to the basics. Hmmm," Mark commented almost in a whisper to himself. "Sounds familiar."

When the service was over, Mark made his way out of the sanctuary but was captured by Randy in the foyer.

"Got a few minutes?" he said. "Pastor would like to see you, well, and all the rest of us, in his office before you go home. Do you have time?"

"Sounds official," Mark said with an unofficial grin on his face. "Sure, what's up?"

"Give him time to make his greetings to the congregation, but we all read your list and are very excited.

He'll get into it more when we all get together. Let's get a cup of coffee."

"Sounds good to me," Mark said, and he followed Randy down the long hallway just outside the one sanctuary wall that led to some class rooms, the church office, and finally ended at the pastor's private office door.

"Hey, good to see you," Chris said, and he stood to shake Mark's hand. All the elders were there, along with a couple of their wives. They were all seated waiting for Pastor Bleeker.

"Didn't get enough of me last Thursday night? I guess it's my turn to buckle up for the ride. Good to see all of you."

Randy, Chris and Mark just fell into a conversation about nothing in particular, and the rest of the group became engaged also in small talk. That lasted for maybe half a dozen minutes until Pastor Bleeker and Barbara came in.

Some of them out of respect started to stand up, but Barbara waved her hand over their heads as she sat down, "Please, it's just fine, relax," she said, "we're not royalty."

"Barbara," Pastor said, "don't knock it. Once they all get to know us, they might not want to stand up for us again," and the whole group laughed. All but Mark, he just shrugged and raised both his hands in a maybe-that's-true kind of way and they all laughed again.

Pastor Bleeker just dove right into his content. "Mark, we have all read your list, and we have all talked about it yesterday morning over breakfast. Sorry you weren't invited. I wanted all their input. To the last one of us, ah, that would include our wives as well, we agree that this," and he hesitated for just a second, "ah, this really is an avenue that we feel needs to be pursued. So much so, that we wanted to talk about how to implement it into our congregation. All we are here today for is to let you know that we are all on board with your list, and to set a time to meet again."

They all looked to Mark for some kind of statement, but he just fell silent leaning forward in his straight back chair with his head down as if he was praying. "You do realize, don't you," Mark said, that anything we ever want to implement into the congregation, has to start with us?" Mark made it a question.

"Oh, of course," almost all of them said in unison.

"What I mean is that if it all starts with us, we have only one of two options to take. Either we get on board *one hundred percent* to apply this, or something very much like this, to each of our personal lives to actively, perpetually pursue as if it were a life changing thing for ME," and he amplified the word me, "to start doing OR, we give IT up and go back to whatever we were doing before. The beauty of making either of those choices, is that as long as we glorify God with any decision we make, then God will still be on the throne of our hearts. So, choosing to proceed, let's say with my list of steps, is the first thing that needs to be established. AND, if that is the decision "WE" are going to make, then that has to start with…" and he stood and pointed to each one in the room. And each time he pointed at any one of them, he said, "you, and, you, and you," until he went around the entire room ending with himself. He

141

then pointed at himself, and said, "I have started to adopt this," and he held up a copy of his list that he had tucked away in his Bible and brought with him to church, "as I was writing it. And truth be known, that list is a result of what I discovered was what I needed to do to be known as one of Christ's true followers, and what I needed to do so that I was equipped to help teach anyone else how to follow Christ. Coming back to basics…" Mark looked at Pastor and said, "I loved your sermon by the way," he inserted mid-sentence, and went on. "It is a basic truth that we can't do anything outside of Christ." And he paused again and finally concluded, UNLESS it is to first get closer to Him. And that set of steps I have outlined is one fantastic way of doing that."

"Okay, Mark, that is why we all are here, don't you know," Chris said. We have all decided that this is our, how did you put it last Thursday night, our next best step? No, we are on board with this, and we just wanted you to know."

"So, are you asking me what our first step should be to proceed?"

"Yeah, I guess it is," Chris's wife commented. "We really do see this as an open door to easily walk through to see people not only come to knowledge of who Jesus is, but how to teach them what their next move needs to be, so we were wondering what you think our next move should be to bring the whole congregation into…" and she paused with a smile on her face, "IT."

Before Mark could answer, he saw that Pastor Bleeker and Randy both, along with their wives, all made a very slight almost imperceptible gesture. It was the equivalent of rolling your eyes at something you did not approve of, only with a lot more tact. He could tell that it was not noticed by anyone else in the room, but it did not escape Mark's acute sense of seeing everything. Pastor Cambridge used to say that he would have made a great detective. Mark looked around and said, "Pastor knows what the answer to that question is. Would you like to tell us?"

Without the slightest hesitation, Pastor Bleeker said in the most kind and humble way, "Mark has already given us the answer to what we are to do next," and he looked directly at Mark before continuing. "Mark, as soon as I read this list, I was on my knees, because I too see this as what I need to do for my walk with the Lord. I have known all these things for ages. I went to seminary, for goodness sake, but applying them on a daily basis is a discipline that will provide two critical things in my life. First, it will set each of my days up to be without confusion, without complaint, without the need to argue, or the need to be right. Secondly, it will open me up to be supremely aware and willing to be available to be seen as one of Christ's true followers. I won't need to show anyone my "pastor's" license, if you will. I am on board with this, and will be, if no one else is. So, to answer that question about how to bring this to the congregation, we first need to complete this individually, and when we do, it will then be time to bring it to all the rest of our congregation."

"Bingo," Mark said, and he gave his new pastor a short thumbs up. "Brothers and sisters, here is my recommendation.

Before there is even a hint of a "WE" on this matter, there has to be a grouping of "ME's." Each of you have been exposed to that list of steps to follow. You are not required to do it. There is not going to be a test in the end, and you won't have an *"attaboy"* taken away from you if you don't do it. There is no penalty for not following through with this list. But if you do, do it by following the steps all the way through, the way it is played out for you. That means taking the time, as I wrote in there, no matter how repetitive it becomes, ALL the way through. Like I said, I made up my mind to do this from the time I wrote it, but I actually didn't start my day-to-day follow up on it until yesterday when I got out of bed. I intend to do this faithfully until I have completed it, and then I intend to insert most all of it into my daily reading and prayers after that. And even more so when life throws me a curve. I will contact you, Pastor, when I am completely finished, or you to me, to talk about our next step then. My advice is simple. If, and I'll say again, if you choose to do this, do it well, and it should take maybe five or six weeks to go through it. Until then nothing, except your prayers for how "WE" may implement it to the congregation after that, should be considered."

When they all left, Mark stayed behind to have a short word with his new pastor. Barbara started to leave, saying, "you guys have your little pow-wow, I'll see you later."

"No, please, Barbara, please stay," Mark asked.

"Okay, sounds very serious."

"It is," Mark said, "but it's also basic, and important. I just want you both to know, that one of the first things that

Pastor Cambridge drummed into my spirit was authority. You are my new authority, Pastor Bleeker, and I intend to follow your lead. I felt led to bring you all that you have seen, and I will pray for you and your decisions. But ultimately, I am to follow your lead from here on, and not only on the implementation for discipleship in the church, but on everything. Well, unless you step completely out of bounds compared to the Word of God, and I have already decided that you won't be going there."

"Mark, I appreciate that, and I will make my head and lead God's Holy Spirit, and I will make myself accountable to the elder board, and my wife of course, which leads me to ask if you would be willing to..."

"Become an elder again? No, not unless you need me, or insist, then of course I will. I know that you have six wonderful Spirit filled elders now. But I will," Mark followed through with, "make myself available to serve wherever and whenever you need."

Pastor smiled, and said, "I know, and I won't push the issue on you. And I do know that you are willing to serve this church."

Goals, Successes, Fears, and it's Easy

The meeting they had in the pastor's office that first Sunday after each member of their leadership received Mark's list, ended well. All in attendance for that discussion included the pastor, Barbara his wife, Randy, Chris and their wives, Mark, and the four other elders, but their wives didn't attend the meeting as they were all waiting in the nursery watching their children. But all who were in attendance for the Thursday night meeting, and who received Mark's list of steps, was sixteen.

Not much was mentioned about the outcome of his list for the next several weeks. Mark did faithfully complete the steps, as well as Martha, he knew, because they briefly touched on it from time to time after church. He also had kept in touch with Pastor Bleeker, who confirmed that he and Barbara had completed the exercise faithfully. Over all Mark thought that there seemed to be a silent reverence that was taking place about it all. When Mark had finished his steps, he called Pastor Bleeker, as he promised he would. He asked the pastor what he thought he wanted to do next, and he told Mark that he really wanted to get the ball, *"rolling, rolling, rolling on the river,"* and he sang it in a pitiful attempt at mimicking Ike & Tina Turner's hit, Proud Mary.

Mark pulled the receiver away from his ear in self-defense. "Pastor Bleeker?" Mark said through his anguish, "Give it up. You may be one of this world's most dedicated pastors, but you will never, and I'll say that again, never make it in Motown."

"You know, Mark, laughter does good like medicine?"

"I do know that, but my problem is am I supposed to laugh, or cry at your musical talent?"

"Oh, that hurts. Aren't you supposed to encourage me?" Pastor retorted.

"Not at the expense of being dishonest," and they both laughed. "Seriously now, any ideas on where to go from here?" Mark inquired.

"Well," Pastor said, "Barbara and I have finished the list, I told you that, but I have been deliberately quiet in asking who else was doing this or who actually finished it. I didn't want to add any pressure. Let me call around and do some investigating, and if there is a good number who are still on board with this, and I honestly believe there is, I'll set up our first meeting on how to proceed."

It was two weeks later when Pastor Bleeker scheduled the first meeting. Once again it was on a Thursday night. That seemed to be the best time for Pastor to be free from all his other duties to get together. When Mark showed up, the room was almost full with several seats that had been put out for all to sit on still empty. After a few minutes, Pastor Bleeker announced that they should begin.

"We're not all here," Mark stated, "or are we?"

"We are all the one who chose to finish the list of steps," Pastor Bleeker said. "Chris, Bob and their wives opted out of it. Their reasons were very understandable. They all said that it was a very good move, and that they would back it, but felt that they were not fitted for it at this time. "So, what we have is twelve of us to move forward with...what shall we call IT?"

"Here's an idea," Randy said. "Instead of a Ph.D., we'll have an Rh.D., *Renewed Hearts for Discipleship.*"

"That's cute," Barbara said, "catchy too. But does it matter what we call IT?"

"Not at all," Mark said, "but we do need to get a little organized," and he looked to the pastor for his leadership. "Do you have an idea about that?"

"I do," he said, "and I have been thinking and praying about that. All of us here have expressed, and have proved our individual desire to become successful at reaching out to our congregation first, and then beyond our walls to work with already confessed believers in Jesus to take the next step in their lives to move onto not only believing in Him, but being a follower of all His ways. I believe this list of steps that has been brought to us is the key. All of us here have crossed that bridge, and here's what I think we can do next. I think it will require three moves on our part to go on from here. First, we need to split up into groups of two. No one couple can be your twosome, though, plus, I think we would be better prepared if we make it men with men and women with women. What we will do is make that one other person your prayer partner, your accountability partner, and your discipleship training partner. I will encourage each of you to periodically go back to steps three and four on that list with each other regularly. Don't be shy, or intimidated by it or each other. That will keep us in tune and keep our enemy away. It will also keep us on track so that this, what was it called, a renewed heart for discipleship, will not fall by the wayside like other programs we have started. The second thing we need to do is meet periodically, and I would suggest every couple of weeks. And that meeting will be for discipleship ONLY. It will not be to complain about anything. Nor will it be for a discussion about anything else. Those meetings can be used to bring names to the table of our own congregation who we will clearly identify as lacking in knowledge of the Word of God, and knowledge of the ways of Christ. It will not be a time of fault finding, but only a time of praying for people, sharing things that we experience, and discussing how we can better befriend someone in need. It will also be a time to confer on who among us might be best equipped to step into a specific situation to start mentoring. That person then will be responsible for praying regularly for him or her, and to report back to the group at the next meeting on progress, or to ask for help if needed. And the third thing we can do, I just brought to light. First is to set ourselves up in twos for accountability. Second is to have our meetings on a group basis, and keep them set aside faithfully for the purpose of discipleship sharing, learning, teaching, and praying. And the third thing is to identify, seek, and assign and pray, and mentor one of our own, to start with, asking God for others outside our farmyard.

"May I add something?" Mark asked.

"Certainly," Pastor said, "what is it?"

"I like everything you came up with, but there may come a time when someone here is assigned to a person to start to mentor, and we find out that it would be better suited for someone else in our group to take over. It needs to be understood that that doesn't mean one is better than another, or that that one person has failed. The second thing I would like to make clear for all of us is that we should never be fooled into thinking that there is anyone who doesn't need to be discipled because they have been a member here since the Civil War. Length of time in the pew does not equate to the assumption that he or she is discipled. In other words, we need to keep our eyes open to become knowledgeable of what they know or don't know, as well as a multitude of other signals."

"Those are very good points, thanks," Pastor said. "And while we're on a roll, I want to talk about some very controversial *WORDS*. Words that can make or break us. Words that everyone on earth has a definition for, and all of them are wrong, unless we are looking at an outcome of these words using the Bible as our guide for definition. I'm afraid it's my turn to make a list, Mark, but I'll just write them on the black board here." He turned around, picked up the chalk and began to scribble three words in very large print. "And these words will not be erased any time soon. We will need to remind ourselves, all of us, of these from time to time." The first word he wrote was…

Goals

"What our goals are, or better put, what our goals should be" he stated, "are critical to understand. And they are not what most people would think that they are. I don't want to get into this tonight. I want all of you to go home, and figure out what you think our goal or goals should be, and bring that back to our first real meeting I have already scheduled for two weeks from tonight, on a Thursday again at 7.

Success

was the second word he wrote on the black board. "Same with this. Our success cannot be measured the same way most measure that. Please come back with your definition of success. And one more."

Fears

"Once again, this is one word that we need to take some real time to talk about. Like the other two words, bring your thoughts on fears." Pastor turned around again and saw that Mark had his hand in the air. Pastor pointed to Mark, who stood and walked up to the blackboard.

"With your permission, Pastor, there is one more word that I would like to bring to the table," and he looked to the pastor for a nod or some form of agreement.

"Go right ahead, Mark."

"Again," Mark said, "I want to refer to Pastor Cambridge's journaling. As I started reading, it quickly became overwhelming. I even had to fight, spiritually that is, through the problem I have had with other churches' doctrines. I discovered that although I have been a follower of Christ for many years, I still needed to come back to the basics on how I can be most effective in helping to disciple others. I discovered just how easy it has always been. I did need to get rid of a lot of **me** to see it, but in the end, I could clearly see how." Then he turned, picked up the chalk, and wrote the word he wanted to bring to them in smaller letters on the black board...

EASY

... "Easy," he concluded as he wrote. "God never made it difficult at all," Mark said turning around again. "What reasons anyone has had to move sideways away from being or becoming His disciple instead of believing only in Jesus as their total end game, is not as important as knowing that they can reverse their direction sideways again the other way. We just need to be faithful to be available to be there for them when they do. To make our goals, to see success, and to eliminate any fear, all we need to do is keep it simple, and two side products from that is joy and peace. God has given us His Word. In there is any and everything we will ever need to know on how to simply *BE* His disciple. With that we will be equipped to know how to go and make disciples. We make it difficult when we think that it is my responsibility to unearth the earthiness in someone, and force them, so to speak, or intimidate someone to act out what we think they ought to be. When that doesn't happen, we are devastated. Our new hopeful then runs away, and we quit. During our training sessions, maybe we can learn how to unload God's responsibility from our clipboards and give that back to Him. We need to understand what our responsibility is, and then be faithful to live that out, trusting God to lead us from that point forward. And, I am here to tell you. It is easy."

Mark sat down and remained silent. He thought that he had said enough during this last week, period, and would let the pastor take over completely.

Pastor took the floor again, "Thanks again Mark, that's good stuff, that is." Pastor concluded with, "If you are all agreeable, I have put together each of you with one other person here to be your partner. I know it would be much more desirable for you to choose your own partner, but by doing this, we will all be just slightly out of our comfort zone, and that will cause us to keep to the exercise, working for its desired effect. It will also be much more beneficial for us all. And I forgot to tell you, we are going to swap partners approximately once every couple of months."

No one had any questions so they all left with hope, but there were some doubts as to whether this was all going to work out, based on their memory of past failures. During the next couple of months, everything seemed to be going well, but every once in a while, one of the team members would call Mark, or Pastor, or Barbara, and even Martha to just check in on, "Are we doing anything at all?" Those doubts were always expelled with a reminder of the definitions for those words, goals, success, fears and easy. They finally understood and agreed on how they were going to live that out. It had been established that they had only three goals. One to be totally ready, like the parable of the virgins spoken of in Matthew 25. The encouragement was to keep enough oil in your lamp that you won't' run out and miss out. The second goal was to pray, wait, and believe that God will bring someone to us to disciple. To be steadfast and believe. The third goal was actually a culmination of the other two…to become one of Jesus' true disciples myself. Fear was defined as anything that kept them from following the pursuit of their goals, or that kept them from believing in how success was really measured. And success, obviously, was defined as not walking away from your goals. We are successful if we are doing what God has shown us to do. The admonishment was to not for a moment shrink back on our laurels, in essence, don't give up, or give in. "STAY STRONG," was the perpetual assignment.

The sensation of success the way the world sees it was additionally provided for them, though, by the fact that over the next few years, their church grew. But not just in numbers, rather in more and more percentages of members who became qualified to mentor and disciple others. Of the original twelve members of the renewed hearts for discipleship team, seven still were still totally active. Some dropped off for a variety of reasons, but each one of them continued to be a solid disciple of Christ, and was active when they could, to go out of their way to help anyone who they felt would benefit from what they had learned. But the real story to be told is that the overall number of the team had grown to eighteen. They still met every couple of weeks, and they still each had one other accountability partner. But the change that had taken place was that discipleship was opened up to the congregation so completely that people were asking for guidance, instead of being asked if they would like to be guided. They also had an outreach to other churches to aid them if they wanted to. Ironically, some of the members of "that other church" began to ask questions that eventually led them back to Pastor Jimmy Lee Cambridge's church where they started from years before. Pastor Bleeker would never hesitate, though, to correct anyone by saying "It's not our church, it belongs to God."

In the years that followed, Mark finally retired from his job and became the main leader for their discipleship team. They had become very organized and lives were being changed frequently. The church, like any church, has its ups and downs, but never do they forget Who is on the throne, and who is not, and they never stop looking for that one someone who would be willing to take the next best step toward becoming one of Jesus' true disciples.

THE END?
Not on your life
Travel with me -- To the Beginning -- And Beyond

Author's notes; Sometimes there doesn't seem to be any easy answers to the things we see in our corrupt world. We are living in a time when most of us Christians have several things that we don't understand. The good news is, that His outcome for you has nothing but good, positive, and wholesome elements attached to your life, once you have truly accepted Jesus as your Savior. Your salvation hinges solely on your belief that Jesus is the risen Son of God, and that he died deliberately to take away your sins, But, if you stop there, not trying to find out what His ways for your life are, you'll miss a lot of His outcome for your life. He is leading you into a closer walk with Him on a daily basis. You are capable, and competent no matter what you may have believed about yourself, to become his active fearless disciple. All you need is the desire to become and stay his disciple. That, then, will prepare you to be capable and competent to disciple just one other person. And, of course, one more. Pray and start to really study what all that means.

PART TWO
To The Beginning

Then he knelt down
and cried out with a loud voice,
"Lord, do not charge them with this sin."
And when he had said this, he fell asleep.

Acts 7:60 NKJ

But You

To The Beginning

10

From the 21st Back to the 1st Century Church

GO!

Pastor Jimmy Lee Cambridge's journaling, which ended up being a record of our society's self-centered ways in the 21st century opened a door that would not be closed again in the hearts of those who read that forty-year block of history. Those journals provided an in-your-face reminder of what had taken place to thwart Christianity in a very short period of time in America, and basically around the world. For Mark, Martha, Pastor Bleeker, and the rest of their church, it was the catalyst used to clearly outline their need to get back to basics if one was to actually take seriously the decree that Jesus gave to his disciples. He told them to *"Go, therefore and make disciples of all nations, baptizing them in the name of the Father and of the Son and of the Holy Spirit, teaching then to observe all things that I have commanded you.* " It was for them, meaning the ones who actually heard Jesus say that in the first century church, a direction that could not be misunderstood or interpreted differently. It was what it was. Clear and precise. "GO!" Jesus said, and that was His last recorded instruction that He gave on this earth. However, as with all of us today, each one of them had to choose if they were going to follow through or not. Can you imagine what our faith would look like today if they just shrugged that command off with, "I don't know. What do you think? Do you think He actually meant for us to do that? I mean, it will put us in a bit of bother, you know with all that talk from the Roman leadership, and even the Sanhedrin. I mean, it won't be easy, will it?" Or, "Do you think that someone else could do that?" Or, "Maybe He didn't mean for us to do that the way we think He meant it." They, like us, carried the same excuse bending, find a way out, heart throb that we do. No, they chose, even unto death for some of them, to take Jesus at his Word. The only difference between them making that choice to follow through or not, and us making that choice now, is that when they made the decision to act on His command in the first century, it could cost them everything. Let me take you back to that first century church, to a time when it really did cost much to step out in faith for Christ Jesus.

WOW

Jesus had been crucified, and all Jerusalem had been affected in one way or another. In fact, much of the known world at the time had been affected, including the Roman

Empire. That's a pretty large impact. Most, however, believed that Jesus was just what the Pharisees claimed he was. A false prophet who blasphemed against God. The Jewish leaders were so steeped in old traditions and teachings that they just didn't understand why God would send someone like this Jesus and not also rid them of their Roman oppressors. That, of course, was just one thing. What really upset the donkey cart was the "grace" concept of God that Jesus taught vs. the "law" side of God that it seemed so often was bypassed by Him. They struggled much, though, with all the miracles that they saw this Jesus do. "I mean, what's that all about?" was the perpetual buzz around all of Judea and elsewhere. "How can a man who said he was sent from God do all those things, without seeking any benefit for himself, not be the real thing?" They remembered the day that He rode into Jerusalem on the back of a donkey's colt. They remembered the crowd singing "Hosanna," and shouting, "blessed is he who comes in the name of the Lord." But the Sanhedrin was not convinced that he was, as the general populous at the time believed, sent from God. They remembered, also, what Jesus said while hanging there on that cross-beam of a torture unit the Romans invented. "Father," He said, "forgive them, for they know not what they do." And to the other one being crucified right next to him he said, "Today you will be with me in paradise." What, they must have pondered, was that all about? "You know," they concluded, "if he really was who he said he was, why couldn't he have just shown us all, and jumped down off that cross, and, and, and." It was those kinds of questions that kept many in

Jerusalem and elsewhere awake at night wondering what they were supposed to believe. And now, just a short time after Jesus' crucifixion, it wasn't only the Sanhedrin who were bending toward the thought that Jesus wasn't who he said he was, but even the general population was wondering if this Jesus really did come in the name of the Lord. But what really started to kill off some of their long-term brain cells of belief, was when his followers claimed that He had risen from the grave. In fact, there were several hundred people, honest people, who they had known for a long time who testified seeing him alive after he was dead and buried. And what about their claim of seeing him ascend into heaven? WOW, and again many, even some members of the Sanhedrin, wondered what they were supposed to believe. And what about all those who did believe that Jesus came in the name of the Lord? They believed what Jesus had told them before He was crucified. That He was the Messiah! So, they followed Him no matter what, although when push came to shove, the really strong ones did run and even deny Him. But that had passed and they now were staunchly proclaiming Him to be their Savior without regard for their own safety. And that was a real problem to the Sanhedrin, because if the followers of "The Way" (that's what they were calling those who follow the teachings of Jesus) are correct, that means that the Sanhedrin murdered an innocent man. Worse, they murdered the Blessed One, spoken of by the prophets, whom God had sent to them. But if the Sanhedrin was correct, they had to ask, "How do we put this rebellion down once and for all?" One could almost hear them debate, "We have to do something, because there are more and more of our brothers becoming believers every day, buying into this Jesus. If this keeps going, all the people will be corrupted, and we won't be able to bring them back around to the real truth of Jehovah." Their concern, and their jealousy, most likely escalated when remembering that there were almost three thousand in one day who converted to the belief that Jesus was exactly who and what he said he was.

So, in Jerusalem, people were being added to the kingdom of God daily, through their faith that Jesus really is the risen Son of God. They believed that He was sent from God, to be sacrificed on the cross, to save them from the penalty due them because of their sins. They were becoming much more knowledgeable about God, and being taught by the disciples about Jesus and that He is the only way to be accepted by God. They were also joyous beyond explanation about life itself. I'm sure that angered the Sanhedrin, and that left almost all of them trying to figure out what their next best approach ought to be. There were some of the Pharisees who were so zealous about crushing all those who were following the teaching Jesus' disciples brought to them, that they were willing to do whatever it took, including producing false witnesses, to put the fire out in the camp of these believers in Jesus.

The battle lines were drawn. The armies on both sides were ready to fight for their cause, although none of the soldiers on either side of the trenches knew much of what to expect. On the one side we see zealots dedicated to following God, with the Law of Moses firmly implanted in their lifelong beliefs.

They were convinced that God did lead their people out of the Egyptians' oppression, and into the land promised to them by God. There was no debate that Moses was God's chosen who brought them the Law. But what of the lower classes who were not as unbending? Many of them also stuck to all that they had been taught all their lives, because it had to be right. The Sanhedrin would not lie to them, and "Well, what else are we supposed to believe?" But there was doubt, and many weren't so sure of what exactly they should believe. This Jesus did put on a pretty convincing act for them to consider. Besides, there were so many who saw things that couldn't otherwise be explained. The ranks of those believing that the LAW was the only correct stance to take, and that Jesus was a false prophet were not in total unison.

On the other side of that battle line, were all the ones who had experienced the truth of Jesus being the risen Son of God. They were willing, although fearful to be sure, that since Jesus really was who He said He was, that they would rather be killed for their new-found faith, than to give Him up. They, for the most part, were unified. Onward they would march to whatever end was in store for them.

Take a walk with me on a path...**To the Beginning**

But You

To the Beginning

11

The Pharisee of Pharisees

Standing in the Front Row, in Total Agreement

As the number of believers grew, the apostles became aware of an issue that was not being managed well among their camps. It was the Grecian Jews who felt that they were not being equally treated, in regards to the distribution of food for their widows. They felt that the Hebraic widows were receiving much better treatment. So, the apostles called all the brothers together and had them elect seven men, full of the Holy Spirit and wise, who would take that responsibility off of the apostles' shoulders, and make sure that all were being treated fairly. And so, Stephen, being one of the seven, proved himself worthy and full of the Holy Spirit, fair, and wise. Many wonders and miracles were seen through him. This continued until he was brought before the Sanhedrin to give an account of his actions and his words. They had brought false witnesses in to testify of Stephen's blasphemy against God. "Are these things so?" the high priest asked him. And to that, Stephen, speaking as the Holy Spirit led, began to give them a history lesson that began with, *"brethren and fathers listen; the God of glory appeared to our father Abraham,"* and his speech ended with, *"You stiff-necked and uncircumcised in heart and ears! You always resist the Holy Spirit; as your fathers did, so do you. Which of the prophets did your fathers not persecute? And they killed those who foretold the coming of the Just One, of whom you now have become the betrayers and murderers, who have received the law by the direction of angels and have not kept it."* When the Sanhedrin heard this, they were furious and gnashed their teeth at him. But he, being full of the Holy Spirit, gazed into heaven and saw the glory of God, and Jesus standing at the right hand of God, and said, *"Look! I see the heavens opened and the Son of Man standing at the right hand of God."* At this they covered their ears and, yelling at the top of their voices, they all rushed at him, dragged him out of the city and began to stone him.

And among them, standing in the front row, in total agreement was the Pharisee of Pharisees. None other than our eminent Saul of Tarsus.

That's the Best Advice You're Going to Get!

"Look, son, I think they're going to stone that man. Can you see?" The boy, maybe twelve years old, stood stretching his neck with one hand on his father's shoulder for leverage. "Yeah, kind of. Why are they going to do that?"

"I'm not sure, but he must have done something pretty bad. They don't stone someone for nothing. In fact, I've never seen a stoning. Wow, I wonder what he did."

"He blasphemed against God!" came the hard condemning voice from the man standing just to the right and in front of him.

"Oh, ah, ah I see" stammered the man softly, and he pulled his son slightly back and away from this small statured, yet intimidating man. "Do you know him?" he asked kind of apologetically.

"I know of him," he answered curtly with disdain, glaring over his shoulder at him. "What's your name?" he asked with the same edge riding on his voice.

"Me, ah, well, my name is Asher, and this is my son Chayim. What's your name? he asked the man, and then continued, "did I do something wrong?"

"Not yet, that I know of, and my name is Saul. What is your interest in this man?"

"I don't have one. We were just passing this way near the outskirts of the city, and saw the crowd. I was just wondering what was going on. What did he do, I mean I know you said he blasphemed God, but how exactly did he do that, if you don't mind me asking?" But no more information was forthcoming. They noticed that there in the midst of this fairly large throng of spectators, was a young man who had been pushed roughly down to the rocks. He showed no signs of worry or fear. The crowd that had gathered was of two ideals, with most of them shouting "Stone him" but some murmured, very quietly so as not to be heard, "Spare him." It was almost a whisper, and it sounded more like a prayer.

"Son, I think I know that man. His name is Stephen." And just as that name slipped from Asher's lips, the angry man in front of him jerked around completely to confront him.

"You know him? I thought you said that you had no interest in him. Are you then, in truth, associated with him? Do you follow The Way, or are you a believer in the one true God?" This Saul of Tarsus almost spat the questions out at this simple, humble being, so that he stepped back as if he had been slapped in the face, while his son's hands shot up over his own face totally awestruck from this verbal attack.

"No, I mean yes, I believe in God. What's The Way?" he asked.

"You said you know him. You even said his name. So how do you know him?"

Asher looked up over Saul's head to get a really good look at the man who was about to be stoned and said, "I think he's the man who came around to my aunt's house to bring her some food after my uncle died. I tried to help her, but I had no extra food to give her. I told her that she could move in with us, but she said that there were these other friends she had who wanted to take care of her."

"Your aunt was a follower of this Jesus, it sounds like, as is this man, Stephen. We feed all the widows, but if your aunt was accepting their help, it must be because she too had blasphemed against God by following The Way. Where does she live?" And again, the question was like a command.

"I don't know. She moved, and wouldn't tell me where she went. She sounded scared, though. But some other people who she hung around with mentioned something about Damascus. Is she in any trouble?"

"You need to watch what you say, and that's the best advice you're going to get today." And with that Saul turned sharply around again ending any further discussion. Asher noticed that many of the men who were going to do the stoning, brought their outer clothing over to this Saul and laid them at his feet for safe keeping. Asher grabbed his son's hand and moved quickly away hoping that they would not be followed, but he had moved only a few feet when he stopped abruptly, listening. He distinctly heard the man being stoned say, *"Lord Jesus, receive my spirit."* Then after a short pause, he also heard him say, *"Lord, do not charge them with this sin."* Asher was haunted by those words for a long time.

So, as Many as Could Leave, Did Leave

On the very day that Stephen was stoned, a great persecution against the followers of Jesus broke out in Jerusalem. When the Sanhedrin broke the mold of restraint on arresting Jesus' faithful, they pulled out all the stops. There were two points that escalated into thorns in their sides. First was the concern that the numbers of new believers in Jesus were increasing at such a rate that the apostles were gaining too much power. But what was really at the bottom line for them, was that they truly believed in the Law given to them by Moses, and the subsequent rules and laws added for the last several hundred years were correct, and that they were being challenged. "It's just not right," I think they believed, "what these disciples of Jesus are teaching, and we're not going to put up with it. The Way is not the way! The Law given to us through Moses is the way. How dare they?" they most likely would continue to complain, "Where did this Jesus come up with all his teachings, anyway? How can anyone really believe that he was seen alive after he was buried? Those witnesses who said they saw him after we know he had died, they have to be liars, and it must have been his disciples who somehow stole his body from the tomb. No other explanation. And it's because of those lies that there are so many who are just rolling over into believing that Jesus was the real Son of God." But there were some in the Sanhedrin who were not so sure of their own stance. Some of the Pharisees really were having trouble not believing that this Jesus was in fact the Messiah spoken of by the prophets of old. So, although some of them did believe, the majority of them did not, and now they were also having a real problem with that apostle, Peter. It was said that he healed a crippled beggar, speaking out with such authority, *"Silver and gold I do not have, but what I do have I give you; in the name of Jesus Christ of Nazareth, rise up and walk."* He got up and walked? What are we supposed to do with that? And what about that other one, John? Both of them were Jesus' disciples from early on, and now they are speaking boldly and openly to the general public about Him." But on one of those occasions, when Peter and John were proclaiming in Jesus the resurrection of the dead, some priests, the captain of the temple guard and members of the Sanhedrin all approached them. Being so upset at what was being said, the officials seized them and took Peter and John away to jail, but because it was so late, they left them there to stay overnight. After bringing them before the Sanhedrin the following day, and complaining about what they were saying in public, they could not justifiably hold the two disciples. So, they ordered them not speak any more in public of the name Jesus. They let John and Peter go. The next day both Peter and John just picked up where they left off continuing to proclaim Jesus to be the risen Son of God. Now, don't you know that left one more ugly taste in the Sanhedrin's self-righteous mouth? They wanted to rid themselves of this problem for good. But it went on and on, so that many more were added to the number of believers, and many wonders and miracles were done in the name of Jesus. Even people from outside Jerusalem came with all forms of sicknesses and hurts, and all of them were healed. The high priest and all of his associates who were members of the San-hedrin were filled with jealousy, so they had the apostles, Peter and John, arrested, and again had them put into public jail. That was that, according to those who vehemently denied Jesus, but that wasn't it at all. Because when they checked on them the next day, they were gone. "Gone? What?" you might hear the high priest say. "Gone? How is that possible? And not only had they escaped through barred cell doors, they were not even flee-ing for their lives! Rather they were out teaching this Jesus again!" They had had enough. Now it was about this time that Stephen was falsely accused, and stoned. And out of that mix of angry, self-righteous and jealous Pharisees came one named

Saul who carried as much loathing for this rebellious brotherhood of Jesus followers as any number of other Sanhedrin members combined. He, with the proverbial pat on the back from the high priest and the rest of the Pharisees, went out to destroy the church. Saul was absolutely relentless. His only interest was to rid the earth of anyone who dared proclaim that this Jesus rose from the dead.

Godly men buried Stephen and mourned deeply for him, but because of the righteous indignation and persecution brought on by the Sanhedrin, particularly Saul, almost all the believers in Jesus, excluding the apostles, were scattered throughout Judea and Samaria.

"What can we do?" many pleaded with each other. "Where are we supposed to go? Just since yesterday when Stephen was stoned, they are after all of us. Have you heard of that one Pharisee, Saul? He seems to be on a personal mission to arrest all who believe in our Lord Jesus. I have heard that he is even going from door to door pulling believers, men and women alike, out into the street and arresting them." Fear, naturally, was in the front of all the believer's minds', especially the new ones. They needed assurance, they needed answers, they needed help, and although the apostles did their best, the followers of Jesus were still left to make one of only two decisions. Recant, and give up Jesus, or get out of town. So, as many as could leave, did leave.

The Saddest Silence He Had Ever Known

"I would have never believed that it would come to this," the man said despairingly to his wife. "If I had, I would have kept you at home. You said you were going to go; I mean did you? Did you go and see them stone, what's his name, Stephen? I heard that some men were secretly persuaded to speak out against Stephen. That they were to testify that they heard him say blasphemous things against Moses and against God. Isn't that the kind of things they said about your Jesus? And I overheard a couple of your friends talking and they said that there were even false witnesses produced who testified that Stephen never stopped speaking against the holy place, and against the Law. It was reported to me that they said boldly before the Sanhedrin, "For we have heard him say that this Jesus of Nazareth will destroy this place and change the customs Moses handed down to us." You know, what I am hearing is only gossip, so I have no way of knowing what is truth. Is what I heard the truth? Was this Stephen falsely accused like they said? Was the real reason they stoned him because of his faith in Jesus? That's what I heard, that they did that just to stop others from following your Jesus' teachings. What, maybe to make an example of him? Or is it true that Stephen really did say those things, and thus deserved to be stoned? And what about you? Do you still think that Jesus is who he said he was? Do you really believe that he was risen from the dead? Huh? Do you? Do you know how much trouble you are putting us in?" He sat down on one of their crudely built handmade chairs and pushed his head into his rough hard worked hands. There was a long pause after which he looked up at his wife who apparently had nothing to say. "My wonderful wife," he began again. "I know you have been taken in with all these, well, outlandish teachings. I haven't complained much about it. I thought it was just a phase you needed to go through. Even I, admittedly, was truly amazed at all the things this Jesus said and did, but in the end, I had to return to earth going back to my roots. What about the Law of Moses? Remember, 'Thou shalt have no other gods before me?' Do you not believe that anymore? You know that most of our friends have packed up overnight and left, or are leaving. They are fearful of what will happen to them, and they should be. But where can we go? We don't have any money, and we don't have anyone, and we don't have anywhere to go. Maybe it's fortunate for us that we never had children. Wow, can't you just stay out of the way for a...."

"Stop, husband," she pleaded softly, as she kneeled on the stone floor of their under-furnished one room house, gently placing her two hands on either side of his face and smiled. She looked lovingly into his angry eyes with a look that spoke volumes of her love for him, leaving no doubt about her understanding for him and her undying desire to be whatever he needed her to be as his wife. There was a "but" in there, and he knew it. "You know that I love you," she continued, "and I would do anything for you that I could do. I also know that your anger is not because you think that I've done something so terribly wrong, but rather because you are afraid of what will happen to me, to us, and I love and respect you for that."

174

"Here it comes," he thought. "Here comes the 'yeah but'. What is she thinking? I don't care as much what she believes in, really, but that she is putting her neck in a noose. Can't she just keep it to herself? What does she expect me to do if she gets arrested? Does she not know that I would rather they arrest me?"

"I can't turn back," she continued emotionally, "and I am even praying for you that you will give your heart to believing that Jesus is the risen Son of God."

"My love," he interrupted her this time, "I have never seen times like this. You know it's not even the Roman guard that we should be afraid of now. It's the Sanhedrin. Actually, it's that Saul. I truly don't understand why we can't just go on the way we were before that day when…"

Suddenly there came a crashing, slamming almost explosive bang on the door. BLAM, BLAM, BLAM. The hit was so violent that both of them jumped to their feet expecting the door to just cave in on them. "Open up," came the command, "I know you're in there. Open up." Amalaha and his wife just stared at each other with a look that each of them totally understood. They knew who it was, but they were powerless to do anything. "OPEN UP," came the repeated order, "and I won't tell you again." Slowly Amalaha stepped to the door and unlatched it, and was going to open it, but he didn't get a chance. As soon as the aggressor at their door heard the latch click, he shoved the door inward with such force that it almost knocked Amalaha off his feet. He pushed rudely into their house, briefly looked down at a list he was carrying, looked at the woman and

175

asked if she was Sama, wife of Amalaha. She slowly lowered her head understandingly, and ever so quietly, almost inaudibly, said "Yes, my lord, I am." One of the temple guards stepped forward at Saul's silent command, and grabbed her roughly and started to drag her bodily out of the opened door.

Amalaha instantly reached out to protect his wife and shouted at the top of his voice, "Leave her alone!" But he wasn't quick enough or strong enough to even slow the man down. Then it was Saul who stepped boldly up to Amalaha, and ordered him to step back, that he was there on orders from the Sanhedrin to arrest anyone, man or woman who believed in this Jesus.

"And, Amalaha, you need to know that although your name is not on my list, it doesn't mean that I won't also arrest you," Saul announced with a cocky kind of confidence, as Sama was being physically dragged outside.

"So, arrest me," Amalaha pleaded. "if you are going to take her to prison, take me with her."

"Do you believe as she does that this Jesus, who was crucified for blasphemy against God, is the Son of God as he claimed, or do you deny him?" And this time Saul seemed to push his chin a little upward as he stepped in a little closer to Amalaha. It looked like a dare, or a hope that he would confess believing in this Jesus. Of course, that would give him one more of his followers to arrest and take to prison. He waited with that smug smile on his face for Amalaha to answer.

Amalaha said nothing for a moment, and then noticed that he had unwittingly grabbed each of Saul's shoulders, and realizing it, he loosened his grip on him, and let go. He looked past Saul to see that they were holding his wife outside seemingly waiting for Saul. "No," he said slowly. "I don't believe that Jesus was who he said he was. What's going to happen to Sama? Can I see her?"

"You know, Amalaha," Saul said, "it's not that hard. All she has to do is recant. She will be punished, of course, but you need to know that this rebellion will have to come to an end."

"Can I see her?" Amalaha said beggingly for the second time.

"Maybe in a couple of days, maybe not." And with that Saul walked out unapologetically. Amalaha followed Saul out into the street where the guards were holding Sama, and saw that there were some others who were also under arrest. He noticed that there were family members and friends of the ones being arrested, like Amalaha, who were pleading, crying, watching their loved ones being taken away. There were also many who appeared to be very angry, but not at Saul. Instead their ire was aimed at the ones being taken to prison, because their hearts were in one accord with Saul against them. Amalaha just stared longingly at Sama, but saw something in her he had never bothered to notice before. She didn't look frightened, or angered, or worried. She appeared to have such peace. He raised his hand for her to see him, and mouthed "I love you, Sama." He stood silently at his door until they were out of sight, and then backed into his house to accept his and her fate. He sat again in that sturdy, yet simple chair to drink in the saddest silence he had ever known. Tears began to fill his eyes at the stillness that filled his empty room.

And the Truth of Jesus Was Being Brought to Everyone

But the church, proclaiming Jesus Christ as Lord, continued to grow, and grow rapidly. Those who were scattered from Jerusalem, for fear of serious persecution, still faithfully preached the Word wherever they went. They had grown bolder, and that boldness aided them to be more fearful of denying Jesus, than of any persecution that they may have had to face. Some of them were first hand believers, meaning that they were the ones who saw Jesus, and listened to His words while He was still alive. They witnessed many things that otherwise could not be explained. Some of them actually saw the risen Jesus. And the rest of those believed what the apostles testified about Jesus' resurrection and ascension. Some of them were there when He was crucified, and testified of what Jesus said at the last before they pulled his lifeless body down off the cross. There was no way that they were going to recant. Onward they marched into cities and towns throughout the entire area. There were others, when hearing the truth from the disciples' testimonies or the apostles' teachings, and seeing the wondrous miracles done in the name of Jesus, who also believed. They were not quite as bold, at first, and did have a sense of dread at times because of persecutions that they heard about. But they too became bolder and bolder. Philip, who being one of the early followers of Jesus, and full of the Holy Spirit, went down to a city in Samaria to proclaim the Christ. When the people of that city heard him, and saw the miraculous signs that he did in the name of Jesus, they paid close attention to what he said. Evil spirits came out of many, and others who were crippled were healed. A great joy was clearly seen in that place. When the apostles heard that the Word of God had been accepted in Samaria, they sent John and Peter to them. When they got there, they prayed for many to receive the Holy Spirit, for the Holy Spirit had not come on any of them. Then when John and Peter had testified of Jesus Christ, proclaiming that they personally saw Jesus risen from the dead, they returned to Jerusalem, preaching the good news of Jesus in many Samarian cities along the way. Philip also continued to preach the gospel in many areas wherever he went. And the truth of Jesus was being brought to everyone in all areas, increasing the numbers of believers throughout the entire region.

All Those Who are Following This Jesus, are Fooled

But Saul was still breathing out murderous threats against Jesus' disciples. An interesting side effect, though, was taking place at the same time. By arresting those who believed in Jesus, and trying to end that rebellion, what actually happened backfired on the Sanhedrin. The number of people converting to the belief that Jesus was exactly who he said he was increased exponentially. "Praise be to God," may have been heard often from all those who were true believers in Jesus their Lord and Savior. God has sent Jesus into the world to save any and all who believed in Him, and no one was going to stop, or even slow that down. That point was even brought to light

179

earlier after the apostles, who had been jailed, were released by an angel and found teaching again of Jesus. They were then brought yet once again before the Sanhedrin to be judged, and some of them were of the mind to have the apostles killed. But one of the Pharisees, a doctor of the law, stood and wisely took issue with the high priest and the other members of the Sanhedrin, and said, "If their purpose is just of themselves, it will die out on its own. You won't have to stop it. But if it is from God, you won't be able to stop it."

Nevertheless, Saul marched on with zeal, to prove not only that the ways of the one and only true God was through the Law passed down from Moses, but also that Jesus was not sent from God as he boasted. The high priest was confident that they, led by Saul, would eventually win out in the end. They hoped there would be an end to any talk of Jesus, whether from their efforts, or as it was put to them, it will die out on its own. They were willing, again, to do anything necessary to bring all those who were responsible for spreading these false teachings to justice. They needed to do something more, they knew, but what that "something more" meant was not exactly known. So, again, it was Saul who stepped up to fill a gap by asking the high priest for letters of authority to take to the synagogues in Damascus "that if I find any, men or women, who are followers of Jesus in Damascus, I may arrest them and bring them back to Jerusalem for justice." So Saul, with his letters of authority, and some others whom he trusted to follow his lead readied themselves for the long journey to Damascus. It was many leagues away, and would most likely take a couple of weeks to complete.

They had to plan their route, and pack whatever they would need for the trek, and Saul was probably over anxious to get started. His heart most likely was filled with excitement for the belief that he would be successful in arresting many for their return to Jerusalem. Saul knew that his efforts were being watched and approved by all in the Sanhedrin, but it wasn't glory he was seeking. Truly, Saul was honestly doing what he believed was the "right" thing to do to honor God. He in no way could accept Jesus, because His teachings, if believed, would in some cases obliterate sections of the Law of Moses, he thought. And he, along with most of the other Sadducees and Pharisees, could not at this time grasp the full message that Jesus was trying to teach. Saul was the staunchest proponent for the destruction of that "Jesus movement." Saul would not, he could not, be swayed from his stance, or his purpose. "It would take a genuine act of God to turn my head," might well have been a statement that could have slipped from the lips of this bigger than life Pharisee, Saul. "How could I ever worship any God but Jehovah? How could I think that there would ever be any other God but Him?" Those are thoughts that Saul could have permanently imbedded mentally, and thus escorted around to be the guide for all of his thinking. He most likely would have thought, "All those who are following this Jesus are fooled, and will certainly regret their beliefs as well as their actions."

Saul, a Pharisee, Dedicated to God - <u>TOTALLY!</u>

Of course, we have no idea what Saul was actually thinking. We only have the Word of God that dials us into the events that took place in the days of Saul, and I compiled all that you read in this chapter from the book of Acts, mainly. We also have Paul's letters, especially the two he wrote to Timothy, to give us insight. Based on those elements, though, we can perceive much. Here's what we can glean from reading about Saul: We see a Pharisee dedicated to God totally, his work ethic is impeccable, and he staunchly stands up for his God. Then, to-the-letter beliefs about the Law given to Moses, Saul heartfully obeyed. His honesty is not in question. Added to that is a list of accolades accredited to him, starting with his ceaseless, tenacious, and unyielding heart-pounding dedication to finish the race. To never quit midstream. That, and more, was Saul prior to Jesus stopping him in his tracks, literally, on his road to Damascus. "Who are you, Lord?" we hear Saul saying. Jesus told him who He was. Try to imagine having lived your entire life under, and believing in, the Law of Moses. Then being trained as a Pharisee, knowing beyond all doubt that it is the only correct stance before God. But then, in less time than it would take you to say the word "conversion", you would be totally convinced of your wrong understanding of who Jesus really is. Although Saul's physical eyes were shut off from light, his spiritual eyes were permanently opened, so that his ceaseless, tenacious, and unyielding heart-pounding dedication to finish the race would be used for the cause of Christ, instead of against Him. That, then, probably gives us a really great description of what it means to be converted. Saul used his two letters he wrote to Timothy to expound on that issue. "But you, O man of God," he told Timothy, "flee these things and pursue righteousness, godliness, faith, love, patience, gentleness." Do you think that God's Holy Spirit is speaking to you and me in that passage today? I do, so that every once in a while, I use those words when conversing with that guy who never ceases to look back at me from the other side of my mirror. "But you," I say out loud to myself, "take hold of the eternal life to which you were called when you made your good confession in the presence of many witnesses." Yeah, I know, but it certainly does require repeating. Be encouraged. Did not God's Holy Spirit also speak to you the day you first admitted believing that Jesus is the risen and living Son of God?

Author's note; There is one truth that in cases is overlooked for its supreme importance. As we read about the conversion of Saul on his road to Damascus, and we believe what we read, we nevertheless often overlook a serious side issue I believe God wants us to grasp. Why is it that God would choose Saul, a self-admitted cleanser of Jesus' followers being absolutely dedicated to ridding his world of Christians, to become the world's greatest proponent for Jesus, then and now? In our humanness, we would want to see a "hero" for Christ step up and destroy the destroyer. But God chose to use the destroyer to destroy the effects of the destroyer, and convert him to become the point man, like a hero, for God's cause of bringing the truth of our Savior to all men and women throughout the earth for all times. Was Saul a "loser" when he persecuted Christians? Was he a "winner" when he converted, and protected Christians? Like so many other important issues God is so faithful to illuminate us with, this one truth holds some great encouragement for me. You see, God's ways are not our ways, are they? I believe what God wants you to see is that no matter what you were, no matter where you have been, no matter what kind of sinner, or user you were, if you give your life to Christ with honest faith alone in who He really is, like Saul did on his road to Damascus, you too can become a Paul type in your surroundings.

But You
To the Beginning

12

I Am Blind, But I Can Clearly See

Who art thou Lord?

Having no other agenda than to exalt God by bringing as many followers of The Way back to stand judgment before the Sanhedrin for their blasphemous ways, Saul was off to Damascus. The journey certainly offered many challenges, with dusty dirty roads, and not having an abundance of food, or maybe lacking the right kinds of food. Sometimes they had to sleep on the side of the road in shifts so that they had someone always alert for fear of wild animals or robbers. "But that is a small price to pay," Saul may have said often, "compared to the prize that awaits us at the end of our journey." Besides, once they were in Damascus, they would be treated with respect at the synagogue where they were to report. They would take time to refresh, eat, get cleaned up and begin their glorious mission.

"This is our fifteenth day," complained Aharon, one of Saul's companions, "you said about two weeks. Sure hope you're right. I really am getting tired of eating all this dust. I mean shouldn't that get us there today? What, maybe this afternoon, or something like that?" He stared at the back of this strict, staunch man leading the way and stepping out as if it was the morning of their first day on the road. "Saul," he said louder. "What are you thinking, that it will be today when we get to Damascus?" He got no reply. Then after a few moments, he began to mumble quietly to himself, "You don't know, do you, Saul the Pharisee? And you don't care either, do you? All you care about is bagging your Christ followers, and you could care less if we even starve, do you? Go on," he continued to mumble softly, "admit it." He was sure that Saul could not hear him, because he could barely hear his own words. So, it came as a shock when Saul turned abruptly around to confront him.

"Yes, I do know. It will most likely be this afternoon, maybe a little later, but definitely before dark when we walk through the gate in Damascus. And you're wrong, I do care, but there is nothing I can do about it. And you are not starving. You ate just today. I know it was a little moldy bread and some cheese, but you are not going hungry. And yes, I am on a mission. I told you that in Jerusalem, that it is important to carry out as soon as possible. Anything else?" Saul stared at the man until he knew that Aharon had been totally embarrassed, then turned curtly back around and kept walking. Aharon looked to his left to get a little comfort from Getzel, one of the other travelers who just shrugged his shoulders and looked away. He turned slightly around to see what reaction he could get from the other travelers and got about the same look. He finally looked straight ahead and concluded that he was going to get no sympathy from anyone. He just breathed a sigh of resignation, but in his heart, he knew that Saul was right. "Of course, he was," he thought. "What can he do? He can't make Damascus suddenly appear, and he can't make food happen." In the end he just resigned himself to his own personal misery, and kept any further statement of discontent to himself. Later that day while on the road, he regained his awesome respect for this man. He and his companions kind of grouped together as they journeyed, while Saul stoically marched on with such confidence a fairly long way in front of them. He appeared, as he always did, like he was planning something.

"You know," Getzel said staring at their Saul, "you have to admire the man. I have never seen a more dedicated man of God ever in my life. I doubt that I ever will. I wonder if he has ever done anything against the will of God. He is the walking Law of Moses."

"I know what you mean," Aharon agreed. "And I'm sorry I complained to him earlier. He is so strict though. But I guess he has to be, you know, carrying all the weight of the Sanhedrin on his shoulders. Anyway, I won't complain ever again while I even suspect that he is within earshot of me."

"How do you know he can't hear you now?" Shumel said with a light chuckle. "The man is amazing, and he has a lot of special abilities. One of them may be extra special hearing."

"No, I know he can't hear us back here." Aharon said with confidence, "We're talking softy enough, and he's, what, I don't know how far up there do you think he is, maybe a couple of hundred feet? It doesn't matter anyway because we're not saying anything negative about him. Really, what I ought to do is speak louder so he can hear, and say something that will let him know we really do respect him."

"No, that would do nothing for Saul." Shumel said nonchalantly, "He never looks for any kind of personal recognition. No, his heart is always simply set on serving God."

"Look," Aharon said, "there's the gate. I can see it just up over that rise. We better pick up the pace."

So, they all walked quickly to catch up with Saul, and when they did, Aharon said with excitement, "Saul, we made it! I can see the gate from here. You said it would be this afternoon. Before dark you said, and you were right. I can't wait to get a change of clothes and some real food to eat. I have been on some other journeys, longer than this one, for sure, but none where it seemed more pressing. I remember one time when…"

"What was that?" Getzel interrupted with a look on his face that replicated only one thing…fear. All of them heard a voice, but could not recognize what it was, or who it was, and they saw no one.

"I don't know!" they all stated at the same time, and all of them rushed forward to Saul. They could not put together what was going on, but they were sure that the voice they heard was coming from somewhere near where Saul had been standing. When they got to Saul, he wasn't standing anymore either; he was on the ground. Not kneeling, or sitting, or laying down, but he had one knee on the ground with his leg tucked up under him, like he had fallen that way suddenly, or maybe had been pushed to the ground. The other foot was flat on the ground, but his body was stretched in an awkward kind of position with his left arm and hand touching the dirt while his other hand was stretched up into the air as if protecting himself from something. His face was turned upward also with his eyes almost bulging out of his head in total surprise. All at once he lowered his head and shut his eyes. He seemed totally astonished, and was trembling. That was a sight that none of them had ever witnessed in Saul before. Then they stepped back suddenly in awe when they heard their staunch, always-in-control Saul speak to someone they could not see… "Who are you Lord?" they all heard him say. Then keeping his same pose, he just seemed to be listening. Was he in shock, they thought? They were all speechless and awestruck themselves. They had never seen Saul like this. Saul seemed to be in a kind of quiet, almost praying mode, and so they just waited. They stared at Saul for a moment, and then looked from one to another hoping to find some answers as to what they should do. Then they heard Saul speak again but there was no one there. "Lord," he said, "what do you want me to do?" There was another long pause after which they all looked to Aharon, as they knew that he was Saul's first choice to lead if some evil had befallen Saul. But Aharon had nothing to say. He just gazed in wonder at Saul who didn't look like he was hurt. He called out many times to him, but didn't even get a nod from Saul.

Finally, "My lord," Aharon said as he kneeled beside his leader. "What is the matter? What is wrong? Are you in pain, or do you need a physician? We are close to the gate now. I can see it from here. It's only a few minutes away. Do you want me to fetch a physician?"

Saul looked up at Aharon, and said very softly, "My friend, you'll need to lead me into Damascus. I have been given a new mission, and I can see nothing at all."

Aharon looked intently into Saul's face and could instantly see that Saul could not see him. He was looking directly at Aharon, but it was obvious that Saul was blind. "My lord," Aharon began, and waved his one hand in front of Saul's face to be absolutely positive. "You can't see me, can you?"

"I just told you that, and I need you to guide me into Damascus, and once there I will be told what I must do."

"Told what you must do? Ah, Saul, ah what do you mean 'told what you must do'?" But Saul said no more about that at that time. And with that, Aharon, being a much larger man, began to scoop Saul up. "Stop," came the mild command from Saul. "I can walk, there's nothing wrong with my legs. I just can't see."

"Where am I to lead you?" Aharon questioned. "Damascus is a large city. Is there somewhere specific you want to go?"

"Yes, there is, and I will tell you as we walk," Saul stated softly. "I'll tell you as we walk," Saul repeated.

So they led Saul by the hand through the gate and into Damascus, and all his fellow travelers were insistent to learn what had happened to their Saul. "Be patient, friends, I will tell you.

Don't worry, I will tell you everything, but for now let me just say that what brought me to the ground like that was the brightest light from heaven."

"What of the voice we heard?" they quizzed.

"I promise I will tell you everything, but for now, just take me into the city," he told them. He looked in the direction of Aharon's face, "We seek a house on Straight Street," he said, "and a man named Judas."

What! Are You Serious?

Saul was unable to see for three days. All who were with him must have marveled at Saul's condition. He neither ate nor drank anything during that time. All those who had traveled with him and others in Damascus, believers and non-believers alike, wanted to hear news upon his arrival into the city. Certainly, all would soon hear everything about this man, who was both admired and feared at the same time, depending on their faith. Those who feared him had a good reason to fear him. They knew what he had been about in Jerusalem, and had been told what he was there in Damascus to do. Those that admired him couldn't wait for Saul to carry out his assignment. Saul wasn't exactly silent during those first few days, but he was mostly in a type of reclusive mood, praying much of the time.

But then on the third day after their arrival, there came a knock on the door. Judas opened up to see a man standing there with a look of extreme confidence on his face. Before Judas could say anything, the man introduced himself. "My name is Ananias," he proclaimed. "I have come to see one whose name was given to me in a vision from God. I am to speak with Saul from Tarsus, may I come in?"

After an astonished look at the man, and an equally awkward bit of stuttering, Judas said, "Sure, ah, absolutely." He was sensing something really big was about to take place, and of course he would not be disappointed. "Please come in," he continued, "I'll fetch him for you." So, he turned and departed from the room through a curtain into one of the inner rooms of his house. "Saul, Saul!" he said excitedly. "Let me lead you to the outer room. There's a man here to speak with you. He knows your name and it seems urgent. His name is..."

"Ananias," Saul finished Judas' sentence, "I know, and he has come to lay hands on me that I may see again."

"Do you know him?" Judas asked.

"Never met him before in my life. But I knew he was coming and I know what he has come to do," Saul said, kind of off the cuff.

Judas was even more dumbfounded than he had been when this total stranger came to his door, seemingly knowing things he couldn't know. He just stared at Saul for a brief moment. Then with that same look of amazement on his face he continued. "I was just marveling at how this man knew to come here to my door in the first place, and how he even knew that you were here, and, and, and now you know all about him. How, what, I mean, where..."

"It's alright Judas, just lead him in here please. I will speak with him in this room."

"Sure, ah, yeah sure," was all Judas could muster for words. So, he turned and pulled back the curtain that led to the outer room and motioned for Ananias to come in. "May I stay Saul? I mean, well, I would really like to stay. Do you mind?"

"I would invite you to stay. Thanks, you have been so kind in letting me stay here, Judas. Yes, please stay."

"My name is Ananias," he said with a little hesitation when he entered the room and turned to address Saul directly, "and I have been told that you too had a vision that I would come to see you."

"Yes, I have, He told me that you would come," Saul announced, and motioned for the man to sit.

"Brother," Ananias continued, "the Lord Jesus instructed me to come and lay hands on you that you may see again, and that you may receive the Holy Spirit." He reached out laying his hands on Saul's shoulders, and immediately Saul could see again. "In my vision, He told me that you are His chosen, and will bring the good news of Jesus to the Gentiles, but that He will show you how much you must suffer for His name's sake."

"I have been waiting for you, and I am grateful for your obedience in following through with what you were called to do," Saul said, relieved.

"When the Lord told me in my vision to come here to lay hands on you, I admit I was not happy about that. I even told Him how I knew of your destruction in Jerusalem and of your intent to do the same here in Damascus. But He told me of His visit that you received from Him on your way here, and also told me to have no fear. You carry a truly fearful reputation for wanting to destroy those of us who believe that Jesus is our Lord and Savior."

There is no accounting as to the extent of their discussion, but I would perceive that Ananias and Saul had a great conversation together. They may have shared testimonies of their conversions, and their thinking on what may be done next. Eventually though, Ananias departed and Saul began to gain his strength. He ate and was refreshed, and he wasted no time in beginning to share the truth of Jesus being the risen Son of God. What a turnaround! Saul came to Damascus with letters of authorization to arrest men and women who now were his brothers and sisters in Christ. He came to knock down Christians' doors to take captive any who would not recant from believing in Jesus, and now he is out preaching in the name of Jesus that He is alive, and is the risen Son of God! He surely shared his story of what happened to him on the way to Damascus with his fellow travelers, and it is probable that they began to believe Saul was not well. We will never know this side of heaven if any of them continued to follow Saul or not. He also began to associate with the believers in the city, and even went to the synagogue and began to preach there about Jesus. "He is the Son of God," he would declare with such confidence. But it was not well taken. When those who followed the apostles' teaching of Jesus heard this, they seriously doubted Saul's intent. "Isn't this the same man who was out to destroy all those in Jerusalem who believed, and is it not this same man who has come here with letters of authority to arrest us? What! Are you serious? And now he is taking the stand that he believes like the rest of us that Jesus is the Son of God, that He in fact is risen from the dead? I just want to stay out of his way!" That was the general consensus of the Christ followers in Damascus. And that wasn't all. The Jews who were not believers, who were waiting for Saul to show up and "take care of business" against the Christians in Damascus, found his altered stance on Jesus not only a disappointment, but also worthy of being put to death. Saul, to them, was now an enemy of the state. So, they conspired to kill Saul at the first opportunity. They had guards placed at all the gates leading out of the city, day and night. If it were up to them, Saul was not going to leave the city alive. But those in the city who knew Saul, and who honestly trusted that he was a genuine convert to believing in Jesus, heard of the plot and warned Saul.

"What are we supposed to do?" they asked one another. But Saul said that he needed to go back to Jerusalem and connect with the apostles there. "They have to know that I now know they were right, and I was wrong. That I have had a vision from Jesus, the one we crucified, and that I am the one He wants to bring the good news to the Gentiles. How can I get out of Damascus without being seen?" Much discussion and planning went into a scheme, where two of the brothers would simply lower Saul over the wall in a basket one night late, and Saul could be on his way. Easier said than done is a statement that comes to mind. It would take a great deal of courage for those chosen to carry out this plan, but that is exactly what they did. So, Saul said farewell to his new friends, his new brothers and sisters in Christ, and found himself once again on the road. We don't know if he made that journey back to Jerusalem alone or not. But wouldn't it make a wonderful story if all of the ones who followed him to Damascus for the purpose of arresting Christians were also converted to following Christ, and were now following him back for the purpose of aiding Christianity?

They Sought to Kill Him

Now, Saul once again found himself in Jerusalem, but posturing from a totally opposite position than the last time he was there. He left Jerusalem on an assignment from the high priest in the Sanhedrin. It needs to be stated also, that the assignment he was given lined up with his personal interest as well. That was to continue his relentless work in arresting Jesus followers in Damascus in the same way he had been successful in Jerusalem. But now, not that much time later, he had no interest in reporting to the Sanhedrin for any success or failure on his assignment, but rather to become part of the ministry with the apostles who were, let's call them, enemies of the state. Saul was now absolutely one of them. The only difference now for Saul in Jerusalem, and when he last left the city, was that the Sanhedrin didn't have a Saul to combat the movement. Worse, now their strict, unbending, uncompassionate dedicated Saul was working just as vehemently for the cause of Christ, instead of against it. So, he was now there to spread the good news that Jesus really was the Son of God, being faithful to make it clear that Jesus actually did rise from the dead. Further, he taught with the apostles that those who partnered with his crucifixion were in fact "dead" wrong about crucifying Jesus. What on earth was the Sanhedrin to do now? But it wasn't an easy move for Saul either. The followers of Christ in Jerusalem, including the apostles, didn't automatically believe Saul. They didn't readily accept his left-to-right turn around stance. It was just a bit too much to buy into. They would need some serious convincing, so they watched and waited. The disciples in Jerusalem were afraid of him, and they had good reason, didn't they? But it was Barnabas who finally took Saul to the apostles and told them how Saul had been visited by Jesus on the road to Damascus, and how Saul had preached with such honesty and power in Damascus in the name of Jesus. So, Saul was accepted and was believed to be a genuine disciple. But the battle wasn't over for Saul in Jerusalem. There were still those who sought to kill him, so that when it was known by the brethren, they took him down to Caesarea, and then sent him to Tarsus. It was during that time we think that Saul studied and gained knowledge about Jesus being the Messiah spoken of by the prophets. It was also during that time that he truly became a dedicated champion ultimately leading to his own death for his Savior. It was during that time that he may have started to become aware, as he was informed by Ananias, just how much he really was going to suffer for the name of his Lord and Savior, Jesus. I wonder if he ever looked back and remembered how really tough he had been toward that innocent man and his twelve year old son standing in back of him the day that they stoned Stephen.

__Author's notes__; The conversion of Saul on the road to Damascus was very dramatic. But the panoramic view of it all illuminates many things. We see God's quality, glory and brilliance. His love, mercy and grace were certainly on display, but equally we see that God's plan wasn't only for the Jews and the Gentiles of Saul's day. It was for all mankind, even to the day you are reading this. We also see two other vital issues. First, anyone, no matter what, can be saved and secondly, we see the importance of following Christ after we are saved.

Look for the difference between being "saved," because of Christ, and being a "follower" of Christ.

PART THREE And Beyond

TODAY

Trust in the LORD with all yor heart,
and lean not on your own understanding;
In all your ways acknowledge Him,
and He shall direct your paths.

Proverbs 3:5-6 NKJ

But You
And Beyond

13

From the 1st Back to the 21st Century Church
(TODAY)

Last instructions to Timothy

The Bible tells us that there was a time after Saul was converted, that the church enjoyed a period of rest throughout all Judea, Galilee and Samaria. I often wondered why that was. Maybe it was because Paul, who was leading the charge against those who stood firm for Christ, was now walking with God in Christ. The church became stronger because of God's Holy Spirit, and it grew with more souls believing in Jesus. They lived in fear of the Lord, not in fear of the Romans or the Sanhedrin. That relative peace was not going to last, for sure. But the benefit of that time when the persecution against the disciples seemed to diminish some, was that a huge growth in the church ensued. The Sanhedrin was powerless to even slow that growth down. That was the beginning of the first century church. Jesus had been raised from the dead, and onward Christian soldiers was the refrain from each believer's heart, although none of them in that time ever heard those lyrics or even hummed the melody. But the beginning of Christ's church on earth had been initiated.

Now years had passed from the time Paul first returned to Jerusalem proclaiming Jesus to be the risen Son of God, to his being known in all of Judea as an apostle of Jesus Christ. He had learned, as the Lord had told him, what he must suffer for the name of Jesus. It would even cost him his earthly life. But he had become just as relentless, with apparently no regard for his own life, for the cause of serving Christ as he had ever been as a staunch Pharisee serving the high priest and the Sanhedrin. Paul never even slowed down for the cause of Christ Jesus. He went on to be an instrument used by God to write powerful letters to encourage, admonish and correct the new churches established in his time. Paul's heart, simply put, was spent giving all that God had given him to the believers then, and because those letters form part of the New Testament of God, all us believers now as well.

Certainly, each of the letters Paul wrote that found its way into the Holy Bible is vital, critical, and is a genuine instruction from our Lord. But it is in 1st and 2nd Timothy that we see the comparison frequently between the ways of the world, and the ways God would have us think, be, talk, act, like, feel, respond, react, as well as what to eliminate, and ignore.

1st and 2nd Timothy, then, are the last two letters to be written by the apostle Paul. At least the last two that were recorded we know of. To the best of my knowledge, *1st Timothy* was written between 63, and 65 A.D., shortly after he was released from an imprisonment in Rome. He starts that letter off identifying himself as, "an apostle of Jesus Christ by the commandment of God our Savior, and the Lord Jesus Christ our hope." He writes this letter to give advice to Timothy on how to better lead the church at Ephesus.

2nd Timothy seems to be the last letter recorded that Paul wrote prior to his execution. He wrote it in 66 to 67 A.D., according to my research, and it is believed that he was put to death maybe in 68 A.D. With the writing of this last letter, I think that Paul was acutely aware of his position. He was in prison in Rome for the second time, and he was awaiting his death sentence to be carried out. He was most certainly weakened physically and most likely emotionally as well. He knew he was coming to the end of his life, and that he was about to be martyred for his unyielding stance for his Lord and Savior Jesus, the Christ of God. But still his heart was bent toward the churches he helped to establish. Still his heart was caring for Timothy. He acknowledges for the last time, *"Paul, an apostle of Christ Jesus by the will of God, according to the promise of life that is in Christ Jesus."* He gives an encouragement to be faithful, telling Timothy, *"You, therefore, my son, be strong in the grace that is in Christ Jesus."* And the letter goes on to give Timothy a trustworthy saying. *"If we died with Him, we shall also live with Him. If we endure, we shall also reign with him.*

If we deny him, He also will deny us. If we are faithless, he remains faithful; He cannot deny Himself." He writes about a workman approved by God. He goes into detail about godlessness in the last days. In there he gives a description that he shares with Timothy as a warning. "But mark this," he writes. *"In the last days perilous times will come: For men will be lovers of themselves, lovers of money, boasters, proud, blasphemers, disobedient to their parents, unthankful, unholy, unloving, unforgiving, slanderers, without self-control, brutal, despisers of good, traitors, head strong, haughty, lovers of pleasure rather than lovers of God, having a form of godliness but denying its power.*" He goes on to say, *"for of this sort are those who creep into households, and make captives of gullible women loaded down with sins, led away by various lusts, always learning and never able to come to the knowledge of the truth.*" Paul knew he was going to be executed, but listen carefully to Paul's last instruction to Timothy. He tells Timothy that all who wish to live a godly life in Christ Jesus will be persecuted. And then he writes, *"evil men and imposters will grow worse and worse, deceiving and being deceived.*" That gives us a really good look at the way things were in those days, and Paul finishes with *"but you must continue in the things you have learned, and been assured of.*"

Paul was Timothy's mentor, and in those letters he wrote to Timothy we see Paul's heart for his *"true son in the faith.*" I think he poured his heart out completely for Timothy to *"endure hardship as a good soldier of Jesus Christ,*" Protect the faith, he said. In essence, he told Timothy, live your life out without regard for what anyone might say or do, so that you, Timothy, might be found worthy of the calling on your life. Paul, throughout those two letters, gives Timothy a glimpse of what was actually going on in the world around them both. But then he gives Timothy instructions many times to follow that which would make the difference between Timothy being a faithful man of God in Christ, or the way others were, by following selfish ungodly worldly concepts. *"BUT YOU, O man of God,"* Paul teaches in 1st Timothy 6:11-12, *"flee these things, and pursue righteousness, godliness, faith, love, patience, gentleness. Fight the good fight of faith, lay hold on eternal life, to which you were also called and have confessed the good confession in the presence of many witnesses."*

There are a few more "buts" to be seen before we travel beyond the beginning, and, of course, the "beyond" I am referring to begins with TODAY. You see, those same letters that Paul wrote that we now know as New Testament books of the Bible, are even more compelling, or should be, than in the days when Paul wrote them. TODAY we have hundreds of more and diverse distractions than were available to anyone in the first century church. So, our need for all those New Testament letters Paul wrote is a large portion, or should be, of our understanding on how to walk through this perverted and corrupted modern age we find ourselves living in. I say should be, but sadly often is not. We are seeing more and more believers adopting a free style, feel-good kind of interpretation of those letters than what was intended. Worse is the reality that much of first and second Timothy is simply being ignored. In many circles sin has become more like mistakes, and being *IN-LOVE* with Jesus isn't heard enough.

Turn Around

Today, many things are much like it was in Paul and Timothy's time. There are similarities in the way we approach life now vs. the way they approached life then. Our preconception about anything, or even anyone, for example is pretty much a human trait, then and now. We see the same separation of classes as they did then, meaning how the wealthy get to live, as well as how and why the poor have to live the way that they do. How we establish what is fair and what is not fair, and who gets to define fairness. Also our faith, our relationships with one another and with God, meaning who is God anyway? That's a fairly common question I think was being asked in the days that Paul wrote his last letter to Timothy, and guess what? I hear that same question being asked from today's populace. There are most likely hundreds of other similarities we could talk about, however, there are also many differences in the "then," and the "now," that control our interpretation of what is right vs. what is wrong, or what is good vs. what is evil. Simply put, it not only comes down to what is normal or what is not normal anymore, but what the definition of the word normal means in the first place. And don't you know that is totally up for whatever "I" think it is. So, once again what gets in the way is our individual depiction of normal. To one, eating a well-done steak is normal and the only way to go, whereas, *"give it to me raw and mooing,"* from another, is normal and the only way to go, just as a simple example. We're all different, aren't we? Well, they were back then too. But today we have, (*I know, I don't like this word either)*, "evolved" from the first century church to include some major differences. The biggest one being how we have come to interpret the Bible, God's Word. We have enveloped Christianity around different ideals, thus the different denominations, thus our teachings, and most importantly the way we teach what Jesus taught his disciples. What *has* become the norm, if you'll humor me a moment, is that our peripheral has become more insightful than what is staring us square in our face. Okay, that is a fairly "normal" human instinct also, isn't it? We all are just human, anyway, aren't we? Well, of course we are, and don't you know that is why God sent His only Son Jesus into the world to save us from ourselves in the first place!

Let me put some additional meat on the table for you. Here are some things that we all need to face doing life now, that they didn't have to face then. Our technology, our social media, and all the increased demands on our money and our time. All of our increased demand for our kids' activities in their school. The need for both parents to work so that the family can live…*comfortably?* Pressure to join, pressure to give, pressure to belong, pressure to be, pressure to please certain family members, etc. And the beat just keeps going on, doesn't it? Just to take you down a short bunny trail though, who do you think is behind all that? But reading again what Paul wrote, "There will be terrible times in the last days," should open our eyes to the world we live in today the same way it was intended to open the eyes of our brothers and sisters of old. The increased evil that seems to just envelope every corner of our lives in some fashion today, should make every one of us Christians stand up and pay attention. That should help us to take the time to see how close "I" am to walking in tune with the teachings that Jesus gave me to follow. If we, meaning us Christians, would spend as much time and energy seeking the face of God for our lives daily as we do to watch the stock market, or the world news, we most certainly would find ourselves closer to what Paul was trying to teach.

It's time that we all turn around, take a deep breath, and examine that, ah, **Me** in the mirror and make some confessions. Not on the "sin" topic in my life, but on the topic of *obeying all that I have taught you,* taken from the last chapter in Matthew. To look at that forgiven person looking back at you who is saying out loud, "BUT YOU, O man, or woman, of God," and for you to hear yourself saying back to him or her, that means "BUT ME."

That's enough, isn't it?

Okay, so here's a really good beginning for all of us in this Part Three section I've titled "And Beyond." Let's stop looking at *the you* in this But You scenario, and begin to look at the **me** in this But You scenario. You see, many years ago, I gave in myself. I remember thinking that it's way past time for me to turn those words Paul wrote to Timothy around to read, "BUT

ME!" When I internalized them for me to take a really good look at my own life in Christ Jesus, I became aware that I seriously needed to put myself in Timothy's sandals and walk my life like it really mattered to Christ. I really did take the time to stare at that man who was woefully staring back at me from the other side of my looking glass. I had to confess that although I truly was a genuine believer in Jesus, I wasn't really interested in actually doing the "following" bit. That doesn't mean that I had some horrible sin that I needed to overcome. It only meant that I had become complacent, or apathetic about God, the Bible and my walk in all areas of my life. But…when the lights finally did get turned on in my life, I instantly saw two things. First, I recognized where I had been, or not been, or should have been to be a true disciple of Christ, and the second thing was why.

In **"The Journal,"** we saw Mark and others struggle with all the same things that all churches struggle with today. The main one, above evangelism, is how to interest true believers who are sitting faithfully in our pews weekly to stand up and grab that golden ring, so to speak, as they are riding on today's comfortable church carousel. To reach out with the desire to touch the lives of other true believers who are not following Christ in their lives. Those who, although are not "bad" people, are never-the-less content to lean on the one fact that "Jesus died for me, I know that I am saved, *and that's enough, isn't it?"* Those who have made no time, and have no intent to learn any more than the basics so that their lives only represent a good person, or maybe a church going person, or maybe both, but do not truly represent being a disciple of Christ.

In part two, **"To the Beginning,"** we read about Paul's faithful, staunch, demanding life as a Pharisee in the first century, and then his miraculous encounter with the Lord. We see, after his bright light meeting with Jesus, he became acutely aware that although Jesus had definitely died, He was now definitely alive. That inescapable truth left Paul instantly converted, and he instantly did a one-eighty in all areas of his life. We read that he made no bones about the fact that since Jesus really was his Savior, there was nothing left to decide. His heart was set to follow Christ, instantly, even onto death, and to take as many with him on that road to saving grace as he could, before he was forced to breathe his last.

In this third section, **"And Beyond,"** you will read chapters that are intended to aid you in seeing the "ME," in the "BUT YOU" instruction, that God's Holy Spirit led Paul to faithfully leave for all to grasp within his first century letters to Timothy. In these next few chapters, you will read about many things that, although are considered *"normal,"* may actually be genuine barriers that have kept you from just rolling over instantly like Paul did. These chapters, most likely, will also include scenarios that, like me, will help you recognize, honestly, what has kept you from standing up in confidence to be counted as a disciple of Christ. My heart and my prayer for you is that after you finish you will have no doubt what so ever what is in store for you next.

Let the last few chapters of this book touch you in such a way that, if you haven't yet become a true disciple of Christ, you will *desire* to begin that process. If you already are a true disciple of Christ, then let these chapters help you to find another to teach. Either way let the words - "BUT YOU, man or woman of God," be an encouragement to you. Study, learn, grow, go and do the same. May the grace of God cover you and enlighten you.

———————————————
———————————————

Author's notes; Saul the Pharisee was lost, but thought not only that he was right with God, but one of only a few who really did step out in faith to serve God with all his heart, mind, soul and spirit. UNTIL he came face to face with Jesus. It was unmistakable for him. He didn't at first know by Whom he was being stopped, but in only a moment, he knew. And when he knew, he didn't try to bargain. He immediately became a disciple of Jesus. He wasn't going to be happy from that moment on to simply admit that he had been wrong, or to be content to just tell people that he now believed what he previously didn't believe. He knew that he not only had to change his path, but that believing wasn't all there was to it. He needed to start to <u>follow</u> the teachings of the One who he confessed was now his Savior in all areas of his life. He submitted himself to the apostles in Jerusalem for training, and to learn. He prayed, and then he stepped up to the plate *and began to teach others. Let Paul and his letters to Timothy lead you to want to do the same. To take the step "**beyond**" being a believer only. To take up your cross daily, and follow your Savior Christ Jesus.*

Be encouraged.
Great things He has done, is still doing, and will do in you, if you are willing.
Be faithful, be at peace, and trust in Him.
YOU CAN DO IT!

But You
And Beyond
14

Christ? Me? The Church?

Going to Church Doesn't Mean…

"Where's that church," Mary asked looking at her internet mapping app. "You know, that old church your grandparents told us about at the reunion? I'm sure they said it was down there just this side of the Third Street bridge." She continued to hunt, and after a few minutes, "Oh yeah, here it is, I found it. Well, I think I found it. If it still is a church. Nowadays you never know. It might have been converted into a convenience store." She laughed and looked over her shoulder at her husband, "Converted. Get it?" she got no response, but kept looking for more information. "Look," she said pointing to some pictures that just came up during her search. "Wow, this thing looks really old. I wonder how old these pictures are. Who knows, maybe they just never took this off the net. They do that sometimes, don't they?" Nothing from her husband. "Don't they Barry?" She turned to face him. "Barry, are you listening?"

"Yeah, sure, ah, the church, converted, sure." Barry nodded half glancing up from his fishing magazine. "What about it?"

"Barry, seriously, tune into this. I want to go there. I want to see the place where they got married. Do you remember all the stuff they told us about their early life in that church?"

"No, ah yeah, I remember," and he made an effort to pay attention. "I do remember. Wonderful stories. Just wonderful."

"You're not interested at all are you? You're just patronizing me. They said that they grew up in that church, and it was a school back then as well, remember? They both went there for their grade school years. That's where they met each other, and then became boyfriend girlfriend, and then dated, and then fell in love, and then, and then, well then, well…then they got married. Isn't that as romantic as it can be?"

"Yes, Mary, that's cool, ah romantic, and I'm not patronizing you. I'm interested in pleasing you, there's a difference," and he put his magazine down. "Honestly, if you want to go, then I want to go for you. And I think it would be very interesting."

"No, you don't," she said back to Barry, "and you are patronizing me. That's okay though, I understand, but…"

"But," he interrupted her, "didn't they say that they got married there, what sometime in the forties? What's that,

214

seventy years ago? How old do you think that church is? They may not even be in business anymore."

"So," Mary said, "what if it was seventy years ago? They're in their nineties. That would make sense. He was in the Second World War, so they must have gotten married after he got home. And actually, the church is over a hundred years old. I just read the bio on this place. That's where I got the pictures, and yes, they still are holding services there. Sunday morning at ten, and I want to go."

"OK," Barry said, "keep your shirt on, but you know they won't know us, and most likely won't remember Grandpa and Grandma either. They stopped going there over twenty-five years ago when they retired and moved to Pennsylvania."

"They might remember them, they might," Mary insisted. "You never know, and besides, maybe we'll want to start attending there."

"Start attending there?" he said with an attitude. "Start attending?" He said a second time to amplify his concern. "Oh, come on," he said throwing his hands up for effect. "You want to start going to church again? What's wrong with our church? I mean if we're really going to start doing Sunday mornings again, why not somewhere we are familiar with?"

"Familiar?" Mary retorted just a little miffed. "We are not familiar anywhere. We only, ever, went there on Christmas and Easter, and stopped that, what maybe seven or eight years ago? Who do you know there now, and who do you think knows us now?"

"Alright, don't get all huffy about it," Barry said, "but why did you say we would start attending that old church? Start attending kind of means going on a regular basis. Is that what you want to do?"

"Maybe," she said. "I've been thinking about it. Ever since Grandma Perkins started telling us about that old church. I think what really got me started was when she told us about how God changed their lives, and it was in that church where they both made their minds up to become Christians. Both of us confessed that too, didn't we?"

Barry leaned forward in his chair. "How God changed their lives? Wait a minute, do you think we need help in our lives? Is that what you are trying to say? What, our marriage?"

There was a way too long pause from her side of the conversation, and then, "Answer my question," Mary said. "Didn't both of us confess to believing in Jesus?" But it came out more of a statement than a question.

"Don't avoid my question," Barry said getting really aggravated.

"Don't avoid mine," she insisted.

"Okay, yeah, we did, but I really need you to answer my question," Barry shot back. "It really sounds like you think we need fixing. Do you?"

Mary stood, took one step toward Barry crossing her arms, "Barry, no, we are not in trouble. I love you and I know that you love me, But…"

"But what?" he interrupted again.

"Barry, we're fine, really, except that I feel like something is missing. Not really between you and me, exactly. We're fine, but, oh I can't put my finger on it. That's why I got really interested in Grandma's stories she told. I think we need to get, well, maybe closer to God?"

Barry relaxed some, leaned back into his chair and hung his head in an unconscious kind of shame. "Yeah, I hear you. Maybe you're right." And for a long time the both of them fell into their own personal think tank of silence. Then suddenly Barry blurted out, "That doesn't mean you have to go to church, does it? I mean as long as you believe that Jesus died for your sins, you're saved. Right? What will going to church do except add more "things" to your life you end up being committed to? We already don't' have time for things we do now. We have seven grandchildren who need us, and mostly on Sunday, I might add. None of them, or our kids either, are going to understand us taking time away from them to go to church," and he puckered those last three words, *"go to church,"* out sarcastically, "are they?"

Mary sat down next to Barry. She gently reached out and placed her hand on his knee. "Barry, we have never had anything to do with our children, or our grandchildren before noon on any Sunday. We can go to church and still be back home by noon." And she just looked up into his eyes, staring right into his heart via his face and waited for a response. And she waited.

Finally, Barry shrugged her hand off his knee, stood up showing off his disgusted side and said, "Look, going to church doesn't mean…."

"We need to go!" Mary sharply interrupted. "Barry, we need to go, and I want to go to that old church."

God's standards

What's in a church, anyway? Who goes, and who doesn't go to church? Why do the ones who go to church go in the first place? Are people who attend church somewhere more in tune with God than people who don't attend church? Are those who have regularly attended church their entire lives more in tune with God and the Bible than those who go to church only on Christmas and Easter? Are God's blessings passed out to those who attend church more than those who genuinely believe, but don't bother to go to church? You know, the questions about "church" don't stop with these few inquiries. And what is more interesting is that there are as many different answers to any one of those questions as there are questions. Our answers will vary, certainly, but in truth our answers should be based on our personal commitment to be a follower of Jesus. The key is to be as dedicated as one can be with a desire to follow the teachings that God has given us from the Bible, without judgment of others. To do that without giving in to the desire to bypass God's Word for "what I think, because it just makes sense." Okay, we all know that, don't we? Don't we?

But let me ask this: Are we more obedient to the teachings of Christ because we go to church regularly, because we tithe regularly, because we give to the needy, because we pray daily, because we are a greeter at church, or even because we are a longstanding officer of our church? Those questions concerning obedience really are more vital than one might think. What we do is important, but trust me on this…**why** we do what we do is much more important. Our obedience ought to be out of love for Him, and what He has done and is doing. And that evaluation needs to be compared with God's standards, not my own, or my church or denominational standards. All the above mentioned "religious" things to do mean little if we are not involved in a personal relationship with Christ. And if we are, we will want to do all those above-mentioned things out of love for Him, and then in obedience to His Word. It then will cease to be a burden to us, but an exercise we will want to do deliberately, in regards to our spiritual walk, every day of our lives.

So, why is it then, that we, the church, have ended up the way we are? And you know what? That is yet another question that will elude a definitive answer, because of the differences between all of us. Some will not even see that we, the church, have ended up in any particular way. "I mean, there are only those who believe, and those who don't believe, right?" Well, sure, that is a point, but that's not all there is to it. There is a lot more to consider, isn't there? Many will see that the reason for our differences is because of the way *"they"* interpret our differences. They, of course, means anyone who doesn't see what I see, the way that I see it. "You know what I

219

mean, don't you? I'm not trying to boast, but honestly our church, denomination, group, has spent years really studying the old manuscripts, and well, you'll have to admit that we are the ones who really do have it right. Right?" Wow! Have you ever heard that? I have! Many, maybe even most, will agree that we ended up *"this way,"* but will define *"this way,"* totally differently than others of us will define *"this way"* as the way we ended up. It can get confusing. Okay, it is confusing. I understand that. If we can bypass the problem of trying to answer each of these questions, and dive right into THE answer, and yes there is only ONE answer to all those questions, it isn't complicated at all.

So, what is the one answer? Glad you asked. You see, the truth is that this debate has nothing to do with who is right or who is wrong. This discussion is dealing with <u>my</u> personal relationship with the Creator of the universe. And yes, you can have one, for those who didn't know that. We all know that we have a great deal of differences. We will all admit that many times something is wrong. It appears, however, that we won't be able to *fix* anything the way that we have attempted to *fix* it up until now. But, also true, is that as long as we try to fix "it," the more "it" becomes elusive. In other words, the "it" that needs fixing is always changing. Key in on the word "always." You see, "it" is elusive because when each of us has an eye on "it," being different than everyone else's "it," we are not keeping an eye ON the one thing that will instantly bypass the need for "it." Keep your eyes, yeah both of them, on our risen Lord, and "it" will not be important enough to give "it" any more consideration. Pray, read and believe His Word, congregate with equal minded believers, and when "it" gets to be too much, pass "it" on to Jesus. Now, I am fairly sure that someone reading this will say, "Oh come on, it can't be that easy, really?" Okay, I'll address that. Yes, it is! All you have to do is give up your right to either know more than you think you do, or your right to be right. You'll hear that a lot in this book. That doesn't mean you are wrong, or that you need to not express your belief, but what it does mean is that you are not letting "your right" dig a hole in your heart that takes your eyes, yes both of them, off of your risen Lord.

What is at stake here, doesn't have near as much to do with the church, per se, anyway. It has to do with you and your understandings of God, Jesus, the Holy Spirit of God, and the Bible. And all that, ONLY, when you have determined in your heart to OBEY what it is that is clearly understandable. And all that, ONLY, when you have determined that you first need, but secondly want to start or keep your personal relationship with Jesus who went to His death on the cross for you.

Just so it is on record, I am certainly a proponent of faithfully attending church, supporting that church, and serving in that church. It is through that relationship that we learn to grow closer to the will God has for each of us, and as a congregation. My point earlier is that God listens to and leads anyone who is a true believer, and a faithful follower of His Son, Jesus, even if they don't go to church regularly. It is most probable, though, that if anyone really is a genuine follower of Christ, they will be a regular attendee in a Christ-centered church somewhere. And "THE" church I keep referring to is defined as any and all true believers in our risen Lord Jesus no matter what church or kind of church they attend. The trick, if you will, is how do we follow Jesus, starting with me, every day outside the church grounds? So, where do we go from here? Well, let me finish Barry and Mary's story. Here's where we left off... *"We need to go!" Mary sharply interrupted. "Barry, we need to go, and I want to go to that old church."*

Barry looked down into Mary's face, and she didn't even blink. He could see that she was not going to give up, but he also saw that she was right. "Okay," Barry said softly sitting back down. "I'll go once, and then we'll see what happens. I do know that I really believe in God, and I really believe that Jesus died for me, so I guess it is past time to find out what else we could, or maybe best put, should do, or be. I've never been comfortable in church, and you know that. I always felt like I was not as clean as some of the rest of them. But then, in a lot of cases, I always felt like I was a lot cleaner than some of them also, so I'm a little apprehensive. I have this feeling that we are going to find out that some of our thinking has been wrong, maybe all our lives, I don't know. But you are right, maybe we should start attending somewhere."

"Thanks," Mary said, "and I am on the same page as you. I believe, and I too have never felt comfortable in church. I don't know what to do next, but maybe we can talk to their pastor to gain some insight for all the things we have had doubts and concerns about. Maybe we'll get some real answers to some of the questions we have had for many years. I guess there

222

is another reason that this has come to my thoughts so strongly now. Your grandmother gave me this Bible. It belonged to her sister and I've been reading it. I've never really read the Bible before, well, all the Bible. You know, Barry, there are some things here that I never knew before. Or maybe I did hear them, but I just always figured that God would let me know somehow if I was ever doing a balancing act on the wrong beam. Now I see that one of the ways He will 'let me know somehow' is with this," and she held up the Bible. There are some other things, also, that I have been reading that don't make sense to me at all. Well, I suppose it is time to find out for sure what is correct or incorrect."

And the story ends the same way so many other stories just like this have ended. After attending that church for a while, they started to learn how God wanted them to live, to think, to respond etc. And it was an unexpected blessing to them when they saw that some of the things that they always believed were correct were actually incorrect, and vice versa. They clearly saw that God's way was not only better, but easier and more pleasing. At first, they thought that in order to become a follower of Christ it meant that they had to give up something that they really didn't want to hand over. But they also found out that there was nothing that they felt they had to give up that hurt at all. In fact, they discovered that some things that they ended up abandoning were replaced with something so much better. But more than anything, they started to experience a peace they had never known before. They began an active prayer life together, and started to make a concentrated effort to invite their family members to join them. They began to tell them how it was God, not only the church, that made the difference in their lives. How learning to be a follower of the teachings of Christ made all the difference in… "how we see things, as opposed to how we want to see things, or expect to see things or how we imagine things must be."

You and I, and every other soul that has ever drawn breath, is a product of our environment. We believe, to start with, only the things that we pick up, call that education if you wish, from every element that exists around us. Some of it is good stuff, and some of it is not. And the confusion sticks its ugly head up early, because what you might have been taught is a good thing, the opposite may be true for me. Many were not raised in a very positive atmosphere, so their learning came from some fairly shady places, or in some situations, no places. Some were not gifted with any positive influences at all. Thus they were forced to survive by figuring everything out for themselves, including what they were supposed to believe. Who we believe in or how we are supposed to live is what all of us have figured out from all those life experiences anyway. But the accuracy of all that is a totally up-for-grabs concept. Depending on your environment, you will have a completely different "this is the way we are supposed to live" explanation than, well, anyone else who has ever drawn breath. So, maybe that would be the best reasoning we can come up with to answer all those questions previously asked up there in this chapter. But, and you just knew there had to be a "but" in here some-where, didn't you? Okay, BUT what I am trying to bring us all to here is not what all the differences between any of us are, but what the one similarity is that connects all of us Christians, of course, that is Christ! Do you not know, do you not believe that the ground is absolutely level at the cross? We all, because we are human, will from time to time want to slip back into rewarding our "fleshly" way of thinking. But the more we deliberately step aside from that charging bull, the more we will spend time checking out "my walk, today, with my Lord." Doing that will give Him more and more control over my thinking and my complaining.

I am just one man. Just one believer who, by the grace of God has turned that corner, and desire greatly, every day, to grow closer to Him. To refresh my walk with Jesus as His disciple, and I have already prayed for you to walk through that open door that God has provided for you.

_____

_____

Author's notes; I can't possibly control all of the I in me, let alone even think about trying to control any of the you in you. But the very best that I will be, from this moment forward will be to do all that I can do to become a faithful disciple of Christ today, deliberately putting down all temptations that would want to make me anything less. The more I study and know God's Word, the more I am willing to follow Christ.

Be encouraged.
Great things He has done, is still doing, and will do in you,
if you are willing.
Be faithful, be at peace, and trust in Him.
YOU CAN DO IT!

But You
And Beyond

15

Metaphoric Perception

Deception Blvd.

There are thousands, maybe millions of us who just love to study people. One of my most favorite things in all my life to do is to watch people. I try to figure them out. Imagine what they might be thinking, what their life is like when no one is watching them. What kind of career they have, etc. It might be when I am sitting on a park bench on a really great warm sunny day pondering the imaginations of those around me. Or I could be striding through the produce department at the super market wondering what that old, and apparently lower income lady over there is trying to figure out. I have been engulfed in this exercise from my earliest memory, even before I gave it any thought. The experiences I have gained from it have taught me so much. But the most valuable lesson I ever learned was that my thoughts and my evaluations were not always correct. Additionally, I became aware that I missed the mark on some matters by a mile. I also found myself, on occasion, issuing an outcome based mostly on my own vain imaginations, and for some it was solely made-up by yours truly. "So," I asked myself, "what was I supposed to do?" I couldn't stop this seemingly useless endeavor. I loved it too much. I tried often to just "put it out of my mind," but that didn't work. There are two things that keep this almost tangible element, of trying to "read" attitudes, activities, and motivations of people alive in my heart, soul and spirit. The first was the fact that the times when I did come up with a one hundred percent correct, right on the nickel evaluation, it produced this awesome feeling in me. The second thing, though, that brought encouragement to me was that I discovered an additional underlying reality in my life when I started to evaluate my conclusions, reading between the lines, so to speak. It was that I have an insatiable desire for truth. It was truth I was really seeking, not correctness for anyone or anything. Rather, for me to be more and more on the right page in my life today, every day. Being on the right page, of course, urged me to seek what truth really was, and not lean on what I thought truth probably was. By studying other characters around me with that new and improved desire, I began to compare what I thought about my own life on any particular topic instead of how it might apply to him, her, it, or them. By God's grace I became more in tune with **myself**. Now all of us are, to some degree, using our imaginations to do whatever. That's a pretty normal activity, and I know of many others who are basically doing the same thing that I have been doing, trying to read people, but their *outcome* isn't, or should I say, most likely won't be anywhere near the same as my outcome. Although it could if they pursued the same path I have tried to walk. Most of them will end up pessimistic, cynical, critical, condemning, angry, jealous, and/or disappointed. Additionally unbeknownst to themselves, their evaluations, similar to the way mine were, are just as incorrect much of the time. But here's the final thing that I discovered about myself when I finally wanted to seek truth, instead of continuing to feed my vain imaginations by trying to figure out what's going on in their minds. I learned that from those who are like I used to be. The longer you pave that path, the more you are convinced of your own invincibility. They become so convinced believing they are so right about anything, that they cease to even consider that they themselves may be wrong. They're just right, no more discussion needed. The more they do that, the more they won't see or listen to correctness at all. They have or will simply believe that they have been gifted with some sort of extra normal powers of perception. They continue on, being more and more convinced of their own superior wisdom, stumbling forward on a path whose street name has to be called Deception Blvd. And, don't you know the reason that I know the name of that street is because my footprints are imbedded in the concrete there. "Okay," you may well ask, "what happened to you?" Well, like I said, by God's grace He showed me two most important postures I, until then, had ignored in my life. While pondering my most excellent

229

ponderings, walking head high and head long down Deception Blvd, I noticed a small dirt path open to anyone, but rarely used, leading off of that main corridor. I was totally content with my "I know that I am one who really does have it all together," attitude, when I looked up to see this small, but very visible street sign that read Truth St. It looked like it led to an obscure one lane, and more importantly, one way bridge hovering precariously over a very deep, fast-moving river that I named Nevermore. I took a chance and stepped out and over that bridge. When I turned around to look back from where I had traveled, I noticed instantly that I could no longer cross back over to Deception Blvd. My eyes were opened and I was no longer blinded by my own vain imaginings. From then on, I began to evaluate everything I felt I needed to evaluate from a totally different standard. That standard has three unspoken background rules. First, to keep from making my lifelong exercise of studying people valid, I had to rid my heart, mind and soul of ANY and ALL judgment what so ever. But at the same time making sure that any discernment that I did come up with for me or anyone else was absolute truth. And finally, I had to simply ignore *it*, doing my best to eliminate *it* from my thoughts if *it* didn't apply to anything that mattered. That last one took some time to correct. So, the next thing that I had to find out was what is real truth? I discovered after a heartfelt search that it had to come from God. That took some time, but with help from some true disciples of Christ, studying the Bible and prayer, all my thoughts, attitudes, ideals, ideas and expressions would come under the authority of God's Word, the Holy Bible. Secondly, relating to not judging, I had to make sure that I viewed myself, daily, as a simple servant of our Holy God, practicing every day to live out the teachings in the New Testament of God, mainly those Jesus taught his disciples to follow. That opened me up to a greater understanding that I also am on a journey the same as everyone else. I just wanted to offer myself as an aid to others, not a righteous condemner of wrong doings. My peace came when I gave up my right to be right on anything. You've heard that before, and most likely will again. But that is a great teach, really. I once heard it said that to be a servant of God is like one standing in His court, not anxious for anything, just waiting for Him to issue instructions to go, stay, walk, sit, rest, run, speak or be quiet and just wait. Then to do all that with confidence, patience, and contentment. My contentment lies in the faith that He is cutting the path for my life, and it's not me who is doing that. It all starts with me doing what I can do each day to know His reality and His truths better as I walk through this life that I am trusting Him to direct.

So, now let me ask you: What do you do when reality steps up, like it did me, and taps you on the shoulder, whispering in your ear, "Hey you, turn around?" And when you do turn around, are you interested in taking the time to search for its truth? Or are you content to tell reality what it is supposed to believe? What do you do when the lights finally get turned on and you see something for the first time, maybe, and it's different than what you thought it would be, or was supposed to be? But here we are again, aren't we? Standing dead center in the debate on one of the most controversial discussions known to any of us in our time. If you're normal, you will question reality back by saying, "Reality? Hmmm, what is real anyway?" and this isn't the first, nor will it be the last time we open that page titled 'interpretation'... But there it is. How do we cross that bridge? What is real anyway? That is what we are here to try to discover. You know Pontius Pilate asked Jesus, "What is truth?" just before he fed Jesus to the ones waiting outside who were yelling "Crucify him!" Much of all the truth that we Christians say we believe in today wasn't accepted by those who asked that question then, including all those standing outside waiting to end the life of our Savior.

Okay, finding out what truth really is won't be the first equation we have to solve. The first ideal any of us Christians need to come to grips with is **how** do we arrive at what is real? So, the first step to discovering what real truth is, and not what my imagined truth is, has to begin with "what is my source of information?" Example...If you watch a video on TV made by someone who is building a deck off the back of his house for the first time, and you watch that video in hopes of learning all you would need to know to build your own deck, you probably will not get the best advice. Conversely, you to go your uncle, Mr. Contractor, and ask him to come alongside you, and work with you to make sure you build your deck correctly. Two things will follow. First, you will have a great deck when you are done. And secondly, you will know how to build another one correctly, or be able to help someone (just like you before you learned) build a deck correctly instead of them relying on some homemade video by an amateur. But here's our human nature again. We, yes me too, start out knowing some things, read a self-help manual, and then figure the rest out for ourselves. Now if you are dealing with a back porch deck, not much harm can come from that. If you do it wrong, you won't have a major problem correcting, and usually the worst-case scenario is that it will cost you a few dollars. Either way, you will learn from that and just keep on keeping on. But take that same principle of figuring it out for ourselves, and apply it to "this is what I know to be truth about God, Jesus, and the Bible," and you know what you will end up with? Well, you are looking at it. Not just our society at large, but our Christian communities in particular. On the whole we, meaning all denominations of believers in Christ, have more ways to "correctly?" build that deck off the back of our house, figuratively speaking, than there are corn fields in Nebraska. Another angle on this evaluation is this. Let's say you were smart enough, in the first place, to seek help building your new deck from someone else, not the video, because you know you are not as experienced as you would need to be to do a really great job. But, instead of going to your uncle, Mr. Contractor, you choose instead to receive advice from a fellow worker who convinces you that he knows exactly what to do. And since you have known him for a dozen years, and he has never lied to you, you say "Sure, I'm putting all my eggs in your basket, buddy." Maybe that will work, or maybe, although he isn't a liar, the truth is that he really doesn't know all that he thinks he does. You and him together find out the truth half way through your build. You, then, may be stuck with a deck not much better than the one you would have ended up with by watching that video…or not. Now again, there won't be much harm done, referencing the deck, but here's another human nature trick of ours. We know where we should go for absolute truth, but rather, we just have to take shortcuts. No? That's not you? Well, that's me and most everyone I know to some degree. But again, expand this second scenario to the next level, regarding knowledge and truth concerning God, Jesus, and the Bible, and, you guessed it. We're back in the corn field.

You see, sometimes it is our vain imaginations that we have chosen to use to prove our "I got this" truths are real. That's like trying to prove that orange juice is made from lemons. Okay, you can remove the word "vain," if you don't like that word, but if you do, you should change the word "sometimes" to "most of the time." Also ask yourself, "Am I basing my reality, my truths, on any kind of selfish or greedy desire?" Wow! and how about this? How honest are we, really? Okay, I believe you are an honest person. I believe our honesty is not at stake here, but our truths may be. Our imbedded truths can be so far away from what is really true, we either don't, or can't recognize it, or we just don't want to. What I am trying to address here, in conjunction to how we arrive at what is real, is *why* we believe what it is that we do believe. That is as vital as *what* we believe. And so back to the beginning, *where* we gather our information to box in our "to die for" beliefs should be a priority.

All of us have many ideas, and some ideals that are solely based on, well, for a lacking of a better way of saying it,

234

"I **think** it's true, therefore it has to be true, right?" So again, I am asking you to make a deliberate move to step out of the corn fields of your life, and step into His marvelous light. That light was given to you to discover your entire life. Just pick up the torch. Stop relying on your own understandings about any truth. Stop figuring it out on your own. And most importantly, stop accepting a truth because, "that was what I was always taught, man." Get back to basics. The Word of God is pure. It is correct, and even though you may not understand it, you will more and more in time. Give yourself over to more prayer time, and associate with godly people.

My heart is in perpetual prayer for all churches. I pray also for all those who have believed on Christ Jesus for salvation. I pray that you will rise above any worldly view of God, and seek with your heart an accurate understanding of all of God's truth.

_____

_____

Author's notes; None of us is, or ever will be, able to call ourselves perfect, but I am seeking to be closer to that every day. I can't do that without God or His Holy Spirit. And I can't even do that without three other things in place. One…a daily humble prayer asking Him to cover me and my thoughts so as to not come up with anything opposite to His ways or thoughts. Two...daily looking into His Word for more direction. And three...seeking to fellowship with like-minded Christians.

Now, I am encouraging you, oh man/woman of God, to do the same. Do it without the <u>need</u> to be recognized by anyone except God. Your number one source of gathering correct information comes from the Book He wrote for us.

Be encouraged.
Great things He has done, is still doing, and will do in you, if you are willing.
Be faithful, be at peace, and trust in Him.
YOU CAN DO IT!

But You
And Beyond

16

"I Know, I Know"

OUCH

Do you remember ever saying to someone, maybe your parents, "I know, I know," when they were trying to inform you of something they felt you didn't know, or more likely something you had forgotten? Or worse, something that you deliberately didn't do that you were supposed to do, or the reverse, something you were not supposed to do, but did? And then looking back on that incident later, believing that in fact you were the one in the know and they were the ones who actually didn't know? OR...are you more like me, where in the end you had to confess, "No I didn't know, I just thought I did." Or was it that you did, but forgot. Maybe you deliberately disobeyed, and that the reason you exhibited the attitude of pushing back with "I know, I know," was because you didn't want to look stupid, or you didn't want to confess that you forgot, or that you really were guilty, and you just didn't want a lecture? Either way, don't we love to look like, or act like, "It's not me who is lacking here, so it must be you." And, of course, following up with that is the additional attitude that shows its ugly head after a long enough period of time. We begin to actually believe the lie ourselves, if not proven beyond all doubt that it really was ME who was bypassing the truth, or reality. And of course, when that happens, we go on our merry way being totally convinced of our supreme superiority. And don't you know that although we may not be aware of it, others may well see our supreme ignorance. OUCH, and again I say ouch. So, now that the questions are posed for you to think about, where do you stand? Is it you who needs to teach me, or are you, like me, ready to see how, why, where and when, "I" can grow some here?

Like Sheep

History teaches us everything we will ever need to know to be able to never repeat any error made by anyone, ever. Think about that for a moment. Is there anything that you have ever failed at, or accomplished for that matter, that someone else hasn't already put an exclamation mark to the same thing, or something very much like it, in one record book or another sometime, or somewhere? So...there you go. Everything falls under that old adage, "If we forget our past, we are destined to repeat it," right? Equally, then, that must also mean, if we remember our past, we are destined to not repeat it. Well surely we all know that, and surely we all pay close attention to that whenever we do or say anything? Ok, so since that has been established and brought to surface again to remind all of us what to do or not to do about anything, ever, all our problems are solved, right? We're good, and any problems we face are just figments of our imagination. We don't need to read yet another author's notes on what is really wrong, who our real enemy is, and most importantly, what we should and easily can do about any spiritual problems we or anyone else faces anywhere, right? Well, if you are one of those thinkers, then both of us are hanging our dirty wash out to dry on the wrong line. I can't speak for you, but I will honestly confess that I am part of our world's problems…Yes, we are. In my life, I have, knowing my past mistakes, ah sins, repeated them. And I have to tell you that I think I am fairly normal. Oh, and destiny doesn't have anything to do with anything, really.

History does teach us much, but the Bible teaches us more of what we need to pay attention to in terms of how we Christians are asked by God to act and react to anyone or anything. The first thing that comes to my mind on this topic is that all of us are like sheep. He goes on to detail that statement by showing us that we are both nearsighted and forgetful. Thus, because of our sin, we are destined to repeat, repeat, repeat, and yet again repeat. All of us, and I am sorry to say, but that includes you as well, have gone our own way. Ok, so where does simply remembering our past to prevent us from doing it all over again come into play? Simply put, all of us have been gifted from the start with free will. That of course means that not only do we possess the ability to choose against what God would want, but we also possess the fleshliness to activate that "right of mine" to achieve what I want instead of what He wants. When it all began in the Garden of Eden, free will was easily controlled with the presence of God to both of the first of our kind. But God wanted to make sure that Adam and Eve wanted to be what He wanted them to be and wanted to do what he wanted them to do, so he gave them a choice without telling them that they were being tested. He developed that test for them to either pass or fail, and oops...here we are. That same test is given to every man and woman born since, including Jesus, who of course was the only One who passed the test. That test is yet again given to all of us believers each day of our lives. Now we do often remember our past, but choose, because of free will, to ignore its consequences. Our overwhelming fleshly desire just needs to be satisfied. We rely instead on God's forgiveness. That then leads us directly into the reason for the need to read yet another author's notes on what is really wrong, who our real enemy is, and most importantly, what we should and easily can do about any spiritual problem. So, I ask, can you think of anyone you know who will profit from reading a book like that? I do, and I'll give you a hint. It's not your boss, or your brother. It's not that obnoxious guy in your church that won't shut up. It's not him, not her, not they, and certainly not them, "BUT YOU." Oh, and of course me too. That is why I am writing all this. It's just for you and me.

Let me step back a moment. Before I gave my life to Christ, I often speculated on why he, she, or they were so far out to lunch about anything. And the "they" was anyone who didn't come close to my way of thinking. What came out of my heart and mind was, "What in the world drove them to do that?" Or, "Where did they come up with that? What, are they blind?" Or again, "Common sense would tell you that that's wrong, what are you, stupid?" and the list of "what's" never ends. I think I could fill a small chapter on additional such statements. Let me ask, are any of those statements ringing a bell for you? Here's a really sad reality. Most of the time in my life when I said those things, I was right on the money. "They," whoever they were, were idiots, or stupid, or selfish, or greedy, or just plain out to lunch. I would almost always end with, "someone needs to put them in their place." Another sad reality is that all those statements, feelings, and condemning attitudes came out of my righteousness, not God's. I knew I wasn't above anyone. You know, along with all my condemning, and all my fault finding came a boat load of "buts" as well. Whenever the finger was, accurately, pointed back at me, I usually had a "but" ready to respond with. Oh, and on that, ah rare, occasion where I could not, out of honesty, deny the accusation being tossed in my lap, I still, at least momentarily, came up with some excuse as to why I was like that, or why I did that. Now, given different circumstances, that last paragraph can be laughed at, because it does define just about all of us. One final sad truth is that there were times that I demonstrated that attitude after I became a Christian. And again, I say that also defines just about all of us.

"What?" I can almost hear someone reading this say to me. "Are you kidding me? Don't you know that the Bible teaches us not to condemn, not to judge? Do you not know that it says that all have sinned? That means you too, you know. Don't you know how horrible it is to do those things after you know the truth? Boy, you really need to watch yourself. How can you write a book like this, and still be guilty of that? I think you need to read your own stuff, buddy. God's going to get you for that. I mean, wow, really wow!" …Hmmm, I see.

So, here's what happened to me. I was a believer in many things from early on in my life. In fact, I don't remember a time that I didn't believe in God. I remember as a child praying that old "now I lay me down to sleep" prayer with my mother. I was taught about Jesus, and how he died on the cross. I was taught to pray every day, and do my best at doing good. I was maybe five years old when I was baptized, and I remember that I had no clue what it meant or what I was doing there, and that was about it. Later on in life, in my thirties, through a series of circumstances, I really did accept Jesus as my Savior and gave my life to Him. I spent many years totally wrapped up in genuinely learning what it meant to be His disciple. I learned two distinct things through that time, and they both are as apparent to me today as then. First is the fact that when the Bible says all have sinned, I know that I am in the front of that line. The Bible goes on to teach that by breaking even one of God's laws, and I did at least that, I was not accepted ever by Him, and that I fell into the same category as the worst of all human beings who has ever lived. Of course that being true, **if** one compares him/herself to God and not to any other sinner. The second fact is that by accepting God's gift, the sacrifice of His only Son, Jesus, I am as accepted by God as much as the best living example of any human being who has ever lived. With that as my daily life belief, I began to paddle up any stream that comes my way today with joy, and not regret. I learned how to stop along the way whenever I was led to do so, and come along side another one of Christ's sheep who is unable to paddle right now. To help them to know how to pick up their oar and row row row their boat again.

BUT…Look out for Traps

As we learn how to row our boat upstream again instead of just drifting down with the current, we become aware that there are serious obstacles we are asked to navigate. So, we do our best to figure out our next best move. Somewhere deep in the recesses of our mind, we sometimes are invaded with the thought, or an unquenchable desire, to be something or someone other than who we are. Something I can achieve, be better at, or different so that I can either fit in, or escape. That is very prevalent today. It is also a signal that identifies that our society is filled with traps. Traps that when looked at in a list can easily be identified, but seem to be ignored when we are hit with one of them on our day-to-day march to our local drugstore. It seems to me, in our current age, there's a never-ending collection of post-it notes hanging on the forefront of our imaginations. Our society has become so engulfed with thousands of items, ideals, books, magazines movies, TV shows, billboards, every form of technology, social media, individualized life styles, selfishness, self-preservation, dog-eat-dog dogma. Earning more money has had to replace career incentives in many cases. How much can I make is now more important than what I want to do for my income. Political maneuvering, men vs. women, and vice versa. Anything foul that can be pushed into our faces has to be accepted, and that list of boulder-size obstacles in our stream we are trying to row against has no limits. We live in a suspicious, obsessed, distrustful, fearful society, and the one I have the sincerest prayer for is the one who cannot recognize that. We all are absolutely surrounded by all of them. Falling into any one of these traps, and it's difficult not to, will almost assuredly prompt either regret, or seclusion in many. So, many live their lives with what they could have been "if only." It's that old coulda shoulda woulda syndrome, and the older we get, the more "but now it's too late" comes into play. Those heartbeats are looking at you from so many fronts in people you see every day, and please pay attention to this next sentence. All that is EVEN coming from many of our dear Christian souls sitting right next to you in your church. Ah, maybe even you? People have always had some regrets, and I think that is fairly normal. We all can look back and see some error in judgment, or some decision we made that brought grief to our life or others in our lives. Traditionally, what we have done with our regrets is confess and ask for God's grace to learn from it. But relate that conclusion to our current world cultures, and normality escapes us. It has turned ugly indeed, and the deception multiplies. One could fill filing cabinets with reasons why that is true, but it doesn't matter at this point. What matters now are two things.

The first is to recognize what has happened to us as a result, and it doesn't take a Ph.D. to figure that out. We have seen a phenomenal increase in suicides, school shootings, and murder in general just in the last decade. An increased desire for young people to not get married, choosing to just live together instead for fear of divorce. And divorce in the last three to four decades has multiplied to unbelievable numbers. We live in a combative society, he's vs. she's, kids vs. adults. Rude isn't rude anymore, "it's just me." My rights are more important than yours, and I'll sue if you don't change your ways. Wanting more for less was where that started, but now it's not just more for less, it's "I want it, you have it, and I don't see any reason why I can't have it, so you have to give it to me." I used to see little old ladies being treated with little to no respect driving their cars, or while shopping in supermarkets. Now I see little old ladies being disgraceful. Okay, I know that you understand, but the second thing that matters is much easier to comprehend and do. If you can *truly believe* what God's Word teaches us in Ephesians chapter six, you know to put on the whole armor of God. This may be a great time to stop and read it. It goes on to teach us why we should do that, so that we can stand against all the fiery darts of the enemy, but more importantly that chapter identifies who our enemy is. And our faith is that he, the enemy, is the real author of all those traps. But, if we as a Christian don't really believe what that is teaching, or worse, don't know or care to learn what that teaches, we can be stuck again and again in one or several of those traps just complaining that "life isn't fair." Okay, here's where you could say, "I know, I know," couldn't you, "but?" You see our knowledge is only one piece of the puzzle. Believing it is another piece of the puzzle, and then acting on it is yet one more piece of the puzzle. The last piece of the puzzle is living out that truth daily, even though you are being placed in the line of fire daily. The really dirty part of that is that all you need to do to be in that line of fire is to simply get up and walk out your front door. Living out another Scripture first may be your next best heartbeat as you grab your oars this morning to row. That would be Proverbs 3: 5-6. "Trust in the Lord with ALL your heart, lean NOT on your own understandings, in ALL your ways acknowledge Him, and He WILL direct your path." That, then, will help us to be in that line of fire without regret. That, then, takes away our need to either fit in or escape. I said that this would be much easier to comprehend and do, and it is, but along with that it can become a most difficult thing to act on or do. The up side of that down side statement is that the only thing that is needed for success is your desire to believe it, and then to step out in it in faith.

I know that you know that too. So why is that so difficult? Good question. You see, it's our flesh that persists in having the last word. We, and yes, I include myself sometimes, just have to end with something like, "that's just not right" speaking about one of those unavoidable traps sitting dead center in my stream making it appear that I can't row around it. "They can't do that!" Or "Why did they do that?" But the closer you get to truly believing in this teach about our enemy, the easier it will get. The less you will be trapped, and God will use you for His glory. Make it your next best ideal to confidently say, "I know, I know," and mean it with an attitude that defines your heart, meaning "I do truly know, and it's me who needs some help here, not them." Lay down the complaints, the malice, and the condemnation about anything, <u>even if you are right about an issue</u>, saying "I know, I know." Pray for them and understand what it means in Ephesians chapter six that they are not your enemy. Understand that they, or the problem, usually will not just disappear because you are right, and they aren't. Start looking at God in your prayers and confessing, "I do know Lord, that I don't need to make any excuses for my actions, ideals, ideas, and anything. I only need to be forgiven, and helped to kindly look at You with thanksgiving when I say "I know, I know."

Author's Note; A really good start for me was when I realized and confessed four things. First, there is more that I don't know, than what I do know. Secondly, the more that I do know, the more I realize what I don't know. And thirdly, the longer I live trying to humble myself before my living God, the greater the distance there was between what I do know and what I don't know. Finally, I realized that of all the things that "I knew, I knew" some of them turned out to be totally unimportant.

Be encouraged.
Great things He has done, is still doing, and will do in you,
if you are willing.
Be faithful, be at peace, and trust in Him.
YOU CAN DO IT!

But You
And Beyond

17

My Private Prickly Box

My goal in this chapter is simple

I went to a writer's seminar once, and the instructor made clear a major point. "Writers, write," he said. "If you want to be a writer, if you want to called an author someday, you just need to write." He went on to say, "It doesn't matter what you write about, or how you write it in the beginning, just write, edit later, but get it down on the page!" Since that time, I have not stopped writing, but through it all I have discovered that there is no topic more thought provoking, for me, or more important for me to write about than issues pertaining to God. Now, the rest of world has a name for all "God" topics. They call them "religion." For me, the idea of religion has been one thought bending ideal after another since I was a teenager. The best definition of religion I have found, before I became a Christian, mostly involved one's own personal belief in who, or what, God really is. Putting that aside for a moment, let me say this. I am not a historian, but based on my long years of study and research, I have come to believe that there is a basic human need to believe in some supreme being who has established the universe, including all of its intricate, even minute, little workings, and most importantly…mankind. Man's spirituality is a genuine concern to most people, interpreted by their individual belief in who or what God really is. Okay, somewhere in the midst of our "oh so gifted" mental powers, is the immense need to seek someone, or something who is responsible for all things. Be it nature, or God, who is ultimately able to have all the answers to every question ever asked. Even those in our societies who strongly profess "there is no God" are still asking the same big question. "Where did all this come from?" They know that the Earth, that is spinning around in space at astronomical speeds with no strings attached, leaves us with a serious line of questions. But those who refuse to even investigate the possibility of a God who "created" it all, are forced to come up with an alternative solution to "Where did it all come from?" Many today, I think more than ever before, are hanging their overall belief system on science, for example. Scientific knowledge has increased exponentially in recent decades because of our tremendous advancements in technology that can aid our scientific experiments to achieve very interesting results. In many circles, though, what we are being asked to do is believe that our technologically advanced scientific world's claims are absolute, and not just theory. Now that's not so bad, as long as it is not being used to destroy solid and firm Biblical truths. In fact, many scientific "facts" prove the Bible. The problem with all that is the same problem that exists in any study on any subject that may force one to trust in "IT" rather than "USE" it as a basis to prove Biblical truths. That then is our first real test. What all of us have to do is either believe that there is a God who has created all things, including science, or believe what some scientists with their advanced technological knowledge are using to prove that there isn't a God who created it all. Of course, if you are in the camp, like me, who does believe in a God who created it all we are placing all those things, including science in the slot where they properly belong. That is, God created those things also, and they are all good for our purpose. Oh, and even if we can't explain it one way or another, we still believe that it's God's creation. That's where faith comes in.

So, how are we supposed to work off of that very fine line between what we think is fact, and what our faith is telling us what truth really is? How do we pick one view we say is true because I have faith that it is, and another that just sounds like it has to true, if they differ? Let's start with one of the most important organs we all have been issued at birth. Our brain. Thinking is what really drives our belief system anyway, isn't it? But relying on anything that absolutely refutes the Bible as the solution to any big question, is ignoring yet another major item issued to all of us at birth. A measure of faith. Faith is the element that ties everything together. Faith was faithfully issued, by God, to all humans so that we have the ability to believe what God is showing us in nature or science, and to be able to believe what God is showing us in the Bible. To simply believe in God. Then, by faith, we can more accurately examine anything, like science, and come to a more definitive response. You see, it's only in the very recent decades that we Christians have even had to answer some of the hardest larger-than-life questions about life, the universe, or even God. Those questions have always been, certainly, but the answers that were commonly available back then provided a more black or white response than we have today. We now have a multitude of seemingly correct, but wrong answers to almost any of those important questions. Adding to that dilemma is the additional misunderstanding about what to believe anyway. The reason for that is because fewer and fewer Christians today don't actually know what the Bible teaches on so many of those larger-than-life questions about life, the universe, or even God.

I can sense someone asking, "So, what do you suggest?" Good question. If you are a genuine believer that Jesus did die on the cross for your sins, and that God did raise Him from the dead, and that He did ascend into heaven like the Bible says, then your faith issue is mostly solved. In other words, if you can get there, you can have faith in anything else the Bible teaches. That doesn't mean that you will understand everything, or that you will have all the answers. It just means that you have chosen to believe that the Bible is accurate, and worthy of trusting. You still will read some things that just don't make sense. Things that you previously struggled with and have put aside to accept something else instead that does make sense to you. Beware of our enemy who is gifted at giving you any alternative to God's Word. Additionally, you will need to be prepared to have to decide between some of those worldly "facts" and Biblical truths. But the more time you spend in actually studying the Bible, checking in with a true long-time teacher of the Word of God, the more your faith will grow. By faith you will need to do that. Consequently, you will be able to differentiate between God's truths and the lies this world is dishing out to you on a golden platter. Sounds like a simple solution, and in truth it really is easier done than said. Here's where I stand. Using science again as just one example of possible things that can mislead me, I'll just say this. I won't have God's Word disproved with any science "facts" especially when those "facts" are being used to prove that there is no God, or that God isn't who He says He is. Neither do I need to disprove any scientific "facts" at all, as long as they don't refute God's Word. I know the battle rages on, but "as for me, and my house, we will serve the Lord."

My goal in this chapter is simple. I am only interested in enlightening you, encouraging you, informing you, and admonishing you on the topics that relate to your faith in God the Father, God the Son, and God the Holy Spirit, and to do that with the help of God's Holy Bible. So, if that's you, you are reading the right book. If that is not you, then you will have a great time learning about all us Christians.

You bet it has!

All that being said, it's time to open the door wide on this Private Prickly Box of ours. You see, even if you understand and agree with these first few pages, there still remains some different explanations for what it means to be a Christian. "How do you know that?" you may well ask. Well, I have been around the block, so to speak, for decades now, ministering God's Word to any number of diverse sectors of our society. I have witnessed that there is a higher-than-it-should-be-by-far percentage of Christians today who have huge deficiencies. This leaves a large number of us living in some degree of disbelief or even fear. Many are combative when asked to defend their faith, not knowing what to say in many circumstances, or simply standing only on their particular denomination or church doctrines. They rely on their pre-designed mission statements or traditions only, rather than on the whole truth of God. And I know that when I say that, many will say, "Well, yeah, what's wrong with that?" They have decided that, basically, "If the pastor said it, that's good enough for me," rather than to recheck what the pastor <u>actually</u> said, or check out what the pastor's real <u>meaning</u> was. But that is only one side of the main issue. We need to be willing to check anything out against the Word of God. Many today have difficulty even being able to defend their faith in Christ. There are a multitude of reasons for that, and I'll dive into that bowl of oatmeal many times in several chapters, but one of the very disturbing truths is that a number of our brothers and sisters in Christ today are in doubt about the accuracy of some well-established, and clearly defined

254

Biblical standards. Please don't look so shocked. That last statement is as real as rain, and I think that most of the reason for that is because of the unbelievable increase in technology, along with the overpowering of our social media. This is where I usually get blasted with "What are you saying, our advanced technology is fantastic…and social media? Come on, don't you know that we are more connected than ever? It's so easy to find out anything, listen to anything, connect with anybody, and all that is good stuff. You know what?" and I hear this a lot in other words, "You're one of those unplugged ignorant Christians who will simply be left out, and left behind. Social media has opened all of us to anyone and everything all the time." And to all that I will say, "You bet it has!"

Okay, so that you don't think that I think there is nothing good about our new and improved technological world, let me take you down a short bunny trail. I will agree, certainly, that not all technology is bad. In fact, mankind has always moved forward with advancing technology. Much of our new world of gadget seeking easiness is great. It betters our lives in many cases. It's important, and even lifesaving. At a minimum much of it is entertaining. All one needs to do is just dig up old memories that go back a few decades in our lives to see just how beneficial our advanced technology has been and is. But there is a percentage of it all, that we, the human race, buys into on a regular basis, not recognizing the evil within it, because we are so plugged in. That hurts. But it isn't all our new technology that I have most of my difficulty with anyway. It's our social media, and the internet in general that I have to draw swords against. Do you not know that at least some of our parenting is not done by us, but by our kid's cell phone groupings? And I am including Christian families as well. We think we are in control because we have placed blocks on their phone and computer to protect them. Truth be known, however, most of our kids are so far ahead of us it makes our heads spin. Even if you have been prudent and done everything you know to do to keep your kids from falling into some of that internet trash, or those really out of bounds social media sites and apps, there are people who don't care, who find ways of grasping our kids' innocence, and bingo, they're infected. But it's not just our kids who view what should not be allowed to be available to view. It's us adults too, isn't it? The things that just "pop up" on our internet are sometimes appalling. Let alone having our personal private computer and phone searching features, that allows any of us to just look for what we ought not to look for. Ouch, I know that hurts, but it is real. What we see, what we feel, what we want, we get. But you see our kids, although they are just like us on that scale, don't have the maturity to put on the brakes. They don't yet have the brakes. So, continue to watch over them, but don't for a moment believe that they don't sometimes have the skills to bypass the blocks you place on their exposure. While you're at it, put some blocks on your own equipment, if you are one who needs that.

So, I am not bashing the idea of cell phones, I am not talking about good or bad parenting. I am not attempting to rid our world of any technology, or the internet. I am, however, attempting to open a window and let some fresh air in beside all of our involvement, mostly in the social media field, because it has and it does generate baggage. And yes, certainly, some good, in all of our lives as well, but it really needs to be looked at. I truthfully have never seen so much time and energy spent by people of all ages, with their heads bowed down, in what arguably can be called worship of their computers or cell phones. I also have never seen a time when there is so much that people seem to believe in because they heard it, or saw it online. It's like this, when someone searches for help on their phone to understand a spiritual or biblical truth, some blindly and unashamedly accept the response they get without any real proof. Now that being said, I am certainly not against using our modern devices as a learning tool. I also am not against social media all together. I am standing up against, like anything else, an overuse of that dusty varmint. A usage that becomes our primary source of truth in place of what the Bible teaches us is truth. Check yourself and pray for God's understanding, for His guidance, for His balance, and yes, for His correction in your usage, and your acceptance of what you see and hear.

Here are two more interesting points I have for us to consider. Here might be a good time for you to ask of me, "Why are you making such an apparently big stink about our involvement and usage of the internet and social media? Don't you know that we already know all that?" And you know what? Again, I say, I am so glad you asked. And again, I say, here's an answer.

First…it doesn't take the greatest of all thinkers among us to see that our world has turned from bad to worse. Many will say, "Come on, it's always been like this." No, it hasn't. Everything that we are seeing today has always been, but certainly not on the level we see it today, and in so many lives we see it in. If you were not aware, I will inform you. We all may be shocked to find out what is really going on with some who are what I might call a closed closet investigator of all things evil. Whatever happened to "Be careful little eyes what you see?" Some, unwittingly, are walking a very ugly path toward destruction. You definitely might be shocked if you knew who is and who isn't on that path.

Consider the phenomenal increase in storage units built and being built in every hamlet across the land from sea to shining sea. We have become a society of "things rule." We are a generation of profound selfishness. "My" rights are more important than truth or honesty. Pornography on demand with the left click of my private computer mouse, is so old now that many consider, "That's just normal, isn't it?" Demands for more money in the work force with little or no education, experience or even a desire to learn. The legalization of marijuana. And the coup de grace? The high number of people, even Christians in many instances, who boldly stand and say, "I don't see anything wrong with all that." I know that I am spelling out the worst-case scenario in some of these examples. My point is that just a few decades ago you wouldn't see anywhere near this kind of conduct that has infiltrated every area of all of our lives.

Secondly, when did we all forget who our real enemy is anyway? The internet, and the users who misuse it, our social media and the users who misuse it, and everything in-between that has captured the core values of so many good people, even Christians, is an outcome of the work being done by the one spoken of in Ephesians chapter six in the Bible. You read about that in the previous chapter. Our downfall is simply that we have relaxed our guard, and we have opened the door to anything that he, our enemy, wished to toss across the table at us. He makes it look like a slice of apple pie alamode, and we just gobble it up. Oh, I know that hurts too, but sometimes the truth does hurt.

BUT…and again I'll say BUT

So, what does all that have to do with anyone's prickly box? And what is a prickly box anyway? Good question. It's a name that I invented for myself to help me, daily, clearly identify not just what I was thinking, doing, acting, feeling, responding, touching, or even what and who I was praying for, but it was my way of helping me understand WHY. It's kind of like setting up a specific place where I would store all my, "I'll think about all that some other time," undesirable attitudes, hopes, fears, and revenges. A place where I put all my "out of sight out of mind" lifelong excuses, ideals, accusations, condemnations, and complaints that I didn't really want to deal with. There were too many issues, too many ways to think about any of them anyway, and I didn't want to concentrate on any one of them, because, well, "I'm not that bad you know."

So, they always just sat there in the background drawing dust, and bending the mental outcome of my life that worked beautifully to destroy not only my joy, but my ministry. Besides, down deep I knew that if I did open up any of those, "I'm the victim here, not them, so I need pity right now" items, I would have to do something Biblical about them. My pride wasn't going to allow that. So, I set up this little heartfelt, mental imaginary capsule to put all of those things in, and I named it applicably, "my private prickly box." What I discovered was an ocean size cavern of reasoning that in many areas of my life didn't match with what God's Word was teaching me to think, or to be. Now my outward actions weren't so bad, you know, by comparison to other Christians…get it? But my heart was so far away from the reality of what a true disciple of Jesus was to be on the inside. By building that prickly box, it was a way to help me not ignore them. It also gave me the benefit of opening only one thing at a time.

Let me give you an example. In chapter 6 of Luke, we read the famous verses, "But I say to you who hear: love your enemies, do good to those who hate you, Bless those who curse you, and pray for those who spitefully use you. To him who strikes you on the one cheek, offer the other also. And from him who takes away your cloak, do not withhold your tunic either." Okay, I know all that. I have even taught all that. I have even helped others walk through all that. In fact, at the writing of this book I am ministering to a man who has been cheated greatly, and wants, almost needs, revenge. I know how to help him get over his desire to go out and purchase a brand-new ball bat to take care of business. BUT…and again I'll say BUT, and here is where the rubber meets the road, as they say. I have been tested on that myself long ago, and although I succeeded in not falling into a trap that I could have fallen into, my heart and my mind were as guilty as if I had. In my thoughts and in my heart, it would come out something like this… *"I can say I love them, and even try to love some of my enemies, but the ones who really lied and hurt me...that's not going to happen. You don't know what they did to me. And I'm supposed to do good to them? Right! I'll send them a card. And how can I be expected to bless those who curse me? Come on, really? Oh, and turn the other cheek? You better be a lot bigger than me, if you slap me on the one cheek. I not only will not give you a second shot, but maybe you need to learn the word… "duck." Also, if someone takes my coat, they certainly won't get my tunic as well. Are you kidding me? They didn't have that right in the first place, and besides that, even if a judge told me to give them my coat, I'm not going to do that. As far as walking an extra mile, it had better be for a good reason. Oh, I might do that, but I'm not going to like it. Why do you need me to do that anyway? And lastly, if you deliberately do something to show me contempt, and despise me, I not only will NOT do good to you, but I will be looking to get even. I might pray for you, but it will only be to have God strike you down. Who do you think I am anyway, Jesus?"* Now that was a bit too harsh, truthfully. I was not that hard hearted, but none the less that was closer to the real state of my heart and mind back then. As I said, I never fell into the trap of not obeying God's edict physically, but often my heart was more like you just read than not. Then, when I did realize that I was a fallen man in my heart as well, I did feel guilty. Even then, I could always be counted on to come up with a respectable excuse for myself because I did the right thing outwardly. And just in case you are not getting this full impact, it was my heart that controlled everything else. So, I continued to flounder, and I continued to be unsuccessful on almost all fronts. My heart needed a revival. By opening my private prickly box with the intent of realizing the real me, I was able to have God completely cure my discomfort and help me to live out His Word, not only preach it.

Lord my God, and I want to be there

But from the time that I deliberately set up my private prickly box for the purpose of really responding to the Scripture that says, "God looks on the heart," I sincerely wanted to figure out a way that I truly would become pleasing in my heart and mind to Him, and not only to be obedient to His edicts. I started to see that what God saw in me was a totally different panoramic view than what I saw in me. I found that I had to look into that private prickly box of mine on a daily basis. Then pray and ask God to reveal to me how HE wanted me to deal with any issue that required my "more like Christ" attitude from my heart, not just my outward action. When I started doing that, I became aware that from that one mental exercise, I could view anything objectively with a pure heart, full of compassion without judging. You see, the old adage applies, "the first step to recovery is confession." Getting there, honestly from your heart, is the only difficult step. In my case, as with you, the confession didn't bring about a belief that I would be even one molecule "worse" than anyone else. We're certainly not "better than" either, but absolutely not worse, because we are not comparing ourselves to anyone else. Only to God and His Word. The confession ends up being simply, "I am not where YOU want me to be, oh Lord my God, but I want to be." I could then pray for help for ME, to see and to overcome MY issues, instead of asking God for help to "fix" them. Then when I did ask God for help for them, it was a different prayer altogether. I would pray for them the exact same way I would pray for myself. That they would see You, oh Lord, and not anything from their private prickly box of undesirable attitudes. It took away my need to be exonerated, my need to hope that "they" would not see my real errors. It extinguished my need to be right, even if I was right. It helped me finally understand what being a disciple of Christ was, beyond looking like a disciple of Christ. It set me free from all the self-condemnation I had going on behind the outward appearance that others saw, or more honestly, what I hoped or thought others saw in me.

So, what do you think? Are you willing to take a can opener to your private prickly box? Good answer, but first let's take a look at what kind of things all of us in our modern times do or think that fills up that prickly box. One warning I would give you is that you don't load something into your private prickly box that truly doesn't belong there. Conversely, though, if you honestly do recognize something that does sit squarely inside your personal private prickly box - Own it! Don't push it to the curb to "think about all that some other time," or it may just end up being an "out of sight out of mind" thing that you may not deal with for another long period of time, or worse, not at all.

Coulda Shoulda Woulda

There are an untold number of items, issues, ideals, thoughts, practices, habits, exercises, hobbies, career choices maybe, or even belief systems in all of our lives, that don't match up with the precepts, or let's say, the ways of God and the Bible. I believe that since we are all sinners, and as we read in the Bible, all have fallen short of His glory, it makes perfect sense that there is none among the living who couldn't desperately need this tool I've named "my private prickly box." A short list of easy to comprehend issues that should end up in anyone's private prickly box may be items like: love of money, time spent with my loved ones, giving to the poor, arrogance or pride, selfishness, envy or jealousy, revenge, unforgiveness, and well, like I said that list really is endless. But this short list is only a start. You see, we all know all these things are barriers that keep us from being all of what God wants us to be. By taking the time to deliberately look at yourself in a mirror without excuses, and admitting whatever your hair-out-of-place item is, will be the key to open your private prickly box. Now, again I'll say this. This is only a tool, but the reason it can work is simple. You will be forcing yourself, maybe for some for the first time ever, to not only admit what you already know, but you will at the same time open the most important door you will ever open. That door is called Humility. God can and wants to heal you of any and everything that is keeping you from desiring to truly follow Him. This is one tool that can help you do that. I've chosen the name of this tool carefully. Private because it's just you and God. Eventually it may lead you to open up with others, but initially, you can be assured that only you and God are working on "it." I chose the word prickly because that's how we need to identify those things that aren't right, but needs to be. They're prickly!

So, let me pick on one issue that I believe all of us need to overcome, and one of the first that I ended up looking at in my private prickly box. WORRY! Most likely, it will be found in everyone's box. So, let's take an expeditionary walk into the world of worry as an example here. The world has had many "bursting at the seams" moments. Like the World Wars, the Civil War in the United States and at different times in other countries as well. Or the taking over of their known world at the time, meting out years or decades of destruction by Napoleon, Stalin, Hitler, Atilla the Hun, and others. Consider some of the Biblical wars and famines or political misconduct, economic recessions, depressions. Or more personal issues, like a family member who has been murdered, been a murderer, or found to be a major drug lord. Divorce, desertion or disease, and that list is endless. We could use our current times for a debate on what should be if..., but the debating about all those issues will only end the same way they always have. With unsolved conclusions, and worrying about any one of them, or several of them will escalate our already destructive worry mode of operation. We could talk about who is responsible for the pandemic, who is responsible for worsening the situation, or who is apt to better heal our nation or world. What our political gain or loss is all about, or what should have happened. Or the great things that have or will happen. Your choice, depending on which standard you are waving above your camp today. If there isn't enough for any of us to worry about in that grouping of titles, how about adding who is right and who is wrong about God? Which denomination preaches the "real" truth, etc. what do you think? Is that enough to worry about? Worry carries no value, though, and we all know that. More often than not, the things we worry about never come to fruition, and when it does, most of the time the outcome is different than we expected. And of the times that we worried and the outcome was exactly what we feared, being the worst-case scenario, worrying about it in the front end didn't alter anything. Worry takes up so much room, creates so much discontent, disappointment, and almost always leads us into a really negative state of, ah, worry, pun intended. Worry is however, one of the most destructive elements in our modern-day habitual imaginations. Furthermore, worry is one of the most popular newsletters we all subscribe to, but, in truth, it should be dropped regularly into another box that I've applicably labeled "shut-up!" But honestly, worry is only one of those tarnished jewels hanging out in our own private prickly box. Its prickly little thorns are just lying there and waiting to tempt you into action. It is saying, "Worry now, figure it out later." It is time, however, for all of us Christians, simply by our faith in the Creator of the universe, to just stop all those debates that plague our conversations, and our thoughts. All those tempers, all those idealisms, and all that energy spent on what coulda, shoulda, or woulda been, if only.... All those issues do need addressing certainly, and we as Christians are not meant to turn a blind eye to any of them. BUT YOU, man or woman of God, take a look at a better, and I will add, the most excellent way to handle worry. Learn how to remove your seat from that controversial table that has to be labeled "the center of contention," and to stop ignoring its seemingly invisible leader. The real head of that table is our enemy. Start right now to pray, but not for "them" first, and not for an outcome of anything first to be "what I just know to be right," but pray first for <u>yourself</u>. Pray that you can walk away from that forum, from that table of contention, whether you are for or against anything, so that God will begin to mentor you to do, to be, to respond to Him first. Another critical thought has to be brought to light. How many of those speeches, those seemingly "correct" ideals, their actions or their stances that we hear daily from so many sources, yes and even the ones you are in agreement with, are based on false doctrines? And could it be, that after much prayer on your part, praying for yourself to see, praying for you to want to follow God's Holy Spirit, that some of those doctrines you previously totally bought into, are not correct at all? That you are really, in your own thoughts, coming from a preconceived understanding of what is correct based solely on what "you think ought to be," and not what actually is? That's because you are an intelligent person, and since you have a caring heart, and because you are honest to a fault, you just know that God would see things your way? Look out! You know, you can't know for sure unless you step back to examine them, and then only with the help of the Holy Spirit of God. Either way, cut the fat called "worry" out of your diet. When you can get your heart right with the Holy Spirit of God, and you will if you submit to HIS teachings, you will then see clearly what false doctrines are being slammed down our throats. And I warn you in advance, not to assume that they are, or they are not, false teachings because of your long term practiced beliefs. Let God lead you. If you do that you will also see that your worry about any of them may have caused you to come up with many wrong suspicions. You will then also see clearly who is really leading those debates, and those divisions. You will then be equipped to "deal" with all of our worldly issues His way, as his new brave ambassador, giving Him right to rule your heart and mind. Your worry level will drop dramatically.

Four-Combination Padlock

Isn't the study of human nature interesting? It really is if you simply start with you. As I have already alluded to, however, dodging road blocks while navigating "worry" street is only one ill-gotten path we all are forced to travel on in our current society. There are so many other issues that you should examine carefully as well. Ones like hatred, total discontent, perpetual complaining, prejudice, diabolical plotting, deliberate deception, greed, sexual impropriety and malicious anger are some of the more recognizable. But there are so many other issues that might be evident if you open that door. Some are mostly hidden from our desire to acknowledge, like being disconnected from family, knowingly lying on your taxes, or petty theft. Holding a grudge against someone, revenge, or jealousy. How about keeping secrets from your spouse, so that he/she can't find out what you spend some of your money on? The truth is that there is no way to count how many other issues there are in need of being tested, that are just silently hanging out and are hidden away. Those issues that are occupying space in our private prickly box will have the greatest opportunity to be eliminated permanently if we deliberately evaluate any of them with a heart honestly crying out for truth.

But there is another truth that shields us from succeeding also from even identifying items in our own private prickly box. That culprit has a name also. I've labeled it "the attitude of my heart." Breaking God's or man's law, or let's say, our personality or character flaws, and maybe all of them combined will account for just a small part of the difficulty in you investigating your prickly little box. There are four important points wrapped up in "the attitude of my heart" that you will need to come to grips with before you are even able to open your box to see what you've jailed inside it in the first place. And this is where it really gets sticky. Enter the word *denial*. Yeah, I know, it's him or her or them who is in denial, not you, right? That's where we get the famous line, "not me, not me." And then of course, the word *interpretation* enters the melee. Another frequent flex to the mix is *excuses*. Lastly enter *extenuating circumstances*. It's like having a four-combination padlock keeping all of your issues carefully protected from, well, anyone, but especially from yourself. Here's a simple example. Let's say you have been told, many times from several sources, that you have an issue with perpetual complaining. Although you may immediately agree that you might have an issue, you, never the less run it through those four examinations. Sometimes, maybe even most of the time, you come up with either a denial, emphatically stating "not-me, not me," or you have a different interpretation for the word perpetual, and therefore releasing the claim, for being misunderstood, or simply that you are being judged. And, of course, no one really understands because…and you add a short list of really good reasons why people think that, but it just isn't so. Or you point out that there are extenuating circumstances that make your complaining understandable, or, you use a combination of the four. Either way, by the time you get done, nothing is looked into carefully, truthfully, or heartfully with the help of God's Holy Spirit to even see if you do have a problem, its severity, or let alone really looking at how you should get help for that issue. Of course there is also the possibility that you, in truth, don't have a problem with that. But you can't know that without investigating it. And investigating it from an on-high perspective. Oh, and by the way, I think that there may be over ten thousand possible combinations in a four-combination lock. And that is why it is so difficult to pin down any one of our real problems, or at least its severity. And that is why it continues to be a problem, and sometimes a real problem that only you don't see that you have. That, then is the reason that we always see someone else's issues so much more clearly than our own. That also is why we see such a vast difference in explaining who or what God really is. And finally, that is why we have differences in our Christian doctrines. WOW! Now, to put you at ease a little, what I have played out for you here in this example, really is a very fair depiction of all of us. Handling that scenario, the way I played it out, is also pretty much human, and yes that includes you, and me as well. So, in conclusion, that is why all us Christians need to stop and do a really intense self-examination, looking deeper than we ever have, individually at first, into the probability that it really is me who stands in the need of prayer, **at least as much** as my worst enemy. By taking that initiative, it will eliminate any thought about what anyone else is doing, should or shouldn't do, think, say or be. This will result in your not adding items to your private prickly box, but actually opening it up with the intent to be healed through that sifting. Start off with these words in your prayer life daily for help from God. "But me, oh Lord." That should be the beginning so that you can clearly see what issues in your life are raising their little hands, saying, "oh, pick me pick me," that you previously didn't see. It also gives God's Holy Spirit an open door to lovingly help you see what needs to happen next for your success in overcoming those newly understood issues you find in your own private prickly box. Remember this: You are not opening your private prickly box for God to see, you are allowing God to open it up for you to see, and to see what and how He wants to help you arrive at the starting gate of your new life in Christ really prepared to run the race for His glory.

Finally...hero to zero to hero

We are flawed from birth, and certainly we all know that. Of course, that is why God gave us Jesus, because He knows that NONE of us will get it right one hundred percent. Well, more honestly, not even close. There is a key, though, to this exercise of opening and examining your private prickly box. That key is so simple, and yet stubbornly, proudly, and even arrogantly ignored more often than not. Humility. True humility is a simple matter of honestly confessing, and being willing to give up your rights for His. To listen carefully, and to seek genuine counsel, understanding that it is your heart that needs repair, not anyone else's. No matter what anyone else is like, has done, or is doing to you or anyone else, it still remains critical that you know that it is YOU who are in need of prayer for yourself. Certainly they, whoever they are, also need humbling, but you can't do that. Only God can, so you need to back off from even thinking about how much they need help, and concentrate all your energies on you and God. And here's a good teach on that. We are all at some time in our lives someone's hero, and yet at some other times in our lives we are someone else's zero. When we are considered a hero, it may or may not be in association with godly issues. The same when we are considered a zero by someone else. Well, that being true, the persons who you consider a zero in your life today are really someone else's hero at another time. But it is God who deals out justice, correction, or rewards, not you. When you totally submit humbly to the way God would want you to see yourself, you will find that joy you have been looking for, no matter what it is that you discover in your personal private prickly box. What you will be doing is opening up your heart, mind, soul, and spirit to hear accurately from the God who gave you Jesus, not only for life eternal, then, when you die, but life now as well. You will then see how easy this exercise is, and how truthfully rewarding it will be. There is no doubt in my mind that you can experience a joy, and a peace you have been missing for a long, long time.

A new and improved prayer life

Now here is a great prayer life starter for you to incorporate. Start your day off with this before you pray for anyone else. Before you ask God's blessings on your day. It will take maybe ten minutes to start with, but then listen when He wants to respond back to you. This is intended to draw you into the presence of God the Father through His Holy Spirit, in the name of Jesus so that you can grow and become His precious working disciple. No matter who you are, where you came from or where you are in life, God can do all this. After setting your prayer life on track with the Holy Spirit of God, take a few minutes each day to look inside your private prickly box.

Start with… "I pray these things, Oh Lord, that you may to be glorified in my life."

I pray for **FRUIT OF THE SPIRIT** to be evident in me. Let my life know and show…Love, joy, peace, patience, kindness, goodness, faithfulness, gentleness and self-control.

SHOW ME, what I did, or said, or thought, yesterday that today I need to do better. Correct me, oh Lord, that I may be known by YOU as your ambassador, then I know that what comes out of me for others to see will bring glory to you.

Help me to lay down all **VAIN IMAGINATIONS**. Show me where my mind really took me yesterday. (Then confess, repent as needed, and ask for help to alter your imaginations today.)

Help me to **CONCENTRATE ON YOU, THE ONE WHO REALLY LOVES ME**. (This will help you to stop feeling inferior, unworthy, and not needed. You are worthy, you are valuable, you are needed. God the Father loves you; Jesus does love you, and the Holy Spirt of God is already showing you that. Listen and believe.)

Help me to **SERVE YOU LORD WITH ALL MY HEART**. Teach me to obey all that you have taught me!

Help me to **STOP JUDGING, OR CONDEMNING** and to let you do the miraculous. Teach me where I might be judging or condemning. Help me Lord to bow before you with complete submission and stop worrying about what anyone else is doing.

GUARD MY MOUTH every minute, Lord, and help me to do the same. Help me to be quick to listen and slow to speak. Lord, remind me that my tongue is like the rudder of a ship. That it can bring life or it can bring death.

I ask that you help me *CORRECT THE ATTITUDE OF MY HEART* to be altered to your desires for me, by the minute, so that others will see You in me, and I WILL give you all the glory.

Help me to *TAKE CHARGE OF MY HOME SPIRIT-UALLY IN LOVE*. My home being all that YOU have placed within my charge, and help me to know how to relinquish authority when it isn't for me to be in charge. That I might love *my wife* as Christ loves His church, or to submit honorably in the way the Bible wants me to submit to *my husband*. Teach me my role as a husband/wife and as a parent so that the rest of my family has the very best opportunity to see You for eternity.

Help me to *MATURE MORE IN CHRIST* every day. That I might be a true minister of your Word, and in doing so will bring glory to You. Let THEM know and remember Jesus, not me.

ALLOW me to have at least one solid man of God or woman of God for a personal brother or sister, that WE may be able to confess, confirm, and share the most intimate things in our lives for each of us to truly become a man of God or a woman of God. And to be an accountability partner in each of our personal prickly boxes.

THIS LAST PRAYER IS HUGE…Help me to **FORGIVE**. I sincerely need help forgiving. So, help me to learn how to forgive any and every one for anything, **BEFORE** it is requested of me, and to lay down all MALICE that my heart may be cleared quickly.

IN THE SAME WAY… Lord, help me to **FORGIVE MYSELF** for everything in my past, and now when I fall, and help me to get up again and start over again and again and again.

Warning

This chapter is for all of us. Read this next text out loud when you are alone, to yourself. *"I should not think that I am above this teach. For even the most knowledgeable, like doctorate degree theologians among us, can be fooled into moving in a direction opposite to God's will. With that as a truth to me, then I admit that I too am vulnerable. I will take heed, then, to study with proven men and women of God about the Bible, about God, about Jesus, and the Holy Spirit of God. And then I will listen and learn to follow HIM."*

Author's notes; *It really is time, in fact way past time, for you to be counted among the overcomers, and not continue to be counted among the group called "overcome." There is a bright light shining in the darkness. That light is the Holy*

Spirit of God, and you are being called.... "Come out from among them," the voice is saying. "Be my true disciple, come join the battle, you soldier of the cross."

Be encouraged.
Great things He has done, is still doing, and will do in you,
if you are willing.
Be faithful, be at peace, and trust in Him.
YOU CAN DO IT!

But You
And Beyond
18

Honesty vs. The Truth

Preface...

This chapter, more than any other by far, zeroes in on "THE" issue as to what, why, and who you may become, in reference to "But You oh man or woman of God." Paul, in many verses throughout the two letters he wrote to Timothy, described the world view of things going on in their time. He encouraged Timothy to run the race, to stay the course. That is my intended effort here. Read this chapter to its end, and cry if you have to, but then rejoice thanking God for all that you may be in Him.

It's freedom, man. Don't you feel it?

There are many truths that will surface as you read this box of tricks, with some of them kicking and screaming all the way up. But there is one reality that has a tendency to spread its wings, to block the corridors of our minds and will require some discussion, before we dive too deeply into the study of Honesty vs the Truth. That is the validation of reality itself. By its very nature, reality should be used to illuminate all dishonesty. Additionally, it usually forces us to admit only all truth. However, in our current world of "it's all up for my inspection and my interpretation" type of thinking, truth has become what I say it is, and because "I don't lie, I know I'm right, and that's that!" That kind of attitude has always existed, certainly, but it has become so prevalent in today's world, infiltrating our masses. It's like an out-of-control misguided missile, arbitrarily hoping for a soft landing somewhere. But in the end, it always self-destructs in some farmer's unseeded wheat field. In many ways it has become the cornerstone for the way we evaluate almost anything we're not sure of. And the most dynamic source we use to gather information we think we need to evaluate comes from our cell phone. We just look up the topic that we are unsure of and that's good enough. We just accept what it gives us, and since we saw it on the net, it has to be factual. Granted that is good enough when we're referring to topics that don't relate specifically to spiritual issues. But I have become aware that many even accept the solution they find on the net about spiritual issues exactly the same way. Now I will also state that there are many great godly sites on the net that we can glean superb information from, but often those sites are not looked for. It is common place for many people to just type in their request and believe whatever comes up. Either way for the most part we are a people who are happy to rely on "what I think is truth, therefore it is truth." We just plug something in that make sense to us. Thus, instead of admitting that "I don't understand," we say "since it makes sense to me, I do understand." We wash our hands of it at that point because we have arrived at a conclusion. The bottom line, then, is that reality gets re-defined, so that, like I said, reality is what I say it is. And the really sad reality that spring boards off of that new and improved way of determining what is real and what is not real, spiritually speaking, is that real reality is left looking for a way back to the interstate. Reality has become twisted to the point, in many situations, where there may only be just a few, by comparison, who stick to their guns, and refuse to accept that "better" way of evaluating. And don't you know, those few, then, are looked on as eccentric, old-fashioned Bible thumpers, or just plain ignorant. It has affected our day to day lives in so many ways, so that we have become suspicious, doubtful, and cautious, thus unable to trust anyone for anything that, well, doesn't make sense to me. And that is putting it very mildly. Now, there are a raft full of reasons for all this, dare I say nonsense? But therein lies the first reality, that defines this age's cultural standards, or let's say lack of godly standards. I think it really does need to be addressed, once and for all. What do you think?

Okay, thanks for your input. Where commonly accepted truths used to be accepted by the high majority of all populations, they are now simply up for grabs. Let's take moral standards, for example. That topic is sitting directly in the center of our behind-the-scenes thoughts anyway. I know, no one wants to talk about morality, and you know why? It's because the meaning of morality has morphed into "whatever I want to make it." Standards are what "I think they ought to be." It's our own personal interpretation of what is moral or not moral. That thinking, because we are all different, will always lead to a debating of the issue, and not a simple discussion of the issue. That debate, then, becomes a contest, and in order for any one stance or belief to be correct, it will require one of the debaters to eventually give in and admit, "you are right, and I am wrong." I can't perceive anyone who is deeply involved in a hard-core debate on the topic of morality being convinced that they are the one who is mistaken. Most people won't even entertain the thought of going through that confessing they are wrong process unless they are absolutely sure that they are, *"and you're going to have to prove that to me anyway, bub,"* added on. Or, they equally don't want to continue to pound on their opponent's contradictory strong hold knowing that they, like you, are not going to give in, so, *"well, we just won't talk about it anymore, but you need to know that your morality is out to lunch, and mine is not,"* may well be the last thought from my heart to yours and vice versa. But openly you may hear, audibly, "No one has a right to tell me what to do!" Therein lies the root for why we can't talk about it, and you know as well as I do that any conversation, ah debate, on the subject of morality is always the elephant in the room that everyone has to ignore. Okay, I get that, and honestly, that is a very correct statement. It truly is an individual choice as to what you think is moral or not moral. You'll get no argument from me on that. Your morality IS whatever you want to make it. I will only say back to you, that you only have that right to choose your morality in the first place because God allows you that as a gift. You see therein lies the real problem. You can choose all day long against what God would rather you choose. He does not, nor did He ever intend to force you to choose His path, or His teachings on the subject of morality. Now, this is where most people who either don't believe in God, or people who do, but don't want to move over into God's court to find out what He says is moral or not, will say, "Great, debate ended. I can choose whatever I want, and that's that, right?" No...certainly that is not that. If you are a true believer in God, in Jesus, and that the Bible is God's Word, you still have the RIGHT to choose whatever you want, but you also need to know that there is a consequence for your choices if you choose to live out your moral beliefs instead of God's, if they are at odds one with the other. Here's where you need to know that I am not your judge. Only God is, but you really should seek Him out to see what it is that He wants, more than expecting Him to honor your choice because you have a RIGHT to choose for yourself. Or that you rely on the fact that since He does love you, then He certainly understands your view, and will give you a thumbs up for it. He won't, and you need to be warned to be very careful how you proceed with that.

So, where should I start? Should I simply hide behind what I am claiming is moral or what I am saying is immoral, keeping my mouth shut because there are so many who don't really want to hear it? That too, is what we Christians sometimes have been asked to do. It goes something like this, "Keep your conservative moral standards to yourself." Okay, so I don't feel that it is fair for me to shut up and sit down when it comes to a discussion on morality, especially when I truly feel that I am standing up for God's morality that has been collected from His Holy Word. Let me ask you a very pointed question. When did our previously understood normal God-approved-by-most-everyone moral ways and standards decide to move south for the winter? Remember, I warned you that some truths will be kicking and screaming all the way up, and of course any talk about morality today will be in the front of that line. And I know that you know, but I am going to shine a flashlight on this anyway. There are many, maybe even most, today who won't see, or who refuse to allow those old-fashioned moral standards to be applicable for today's life styles. Did you not know that those old-fashioned moral standards were derived from godly, Biblical standards, in the first place? In order to make them not applicable, one has to disavow what the Bible says. Or you could just choose to believe that "that part" meaning the thing you don't like, "of God's Word has been corrupted." And that in truth, "some man wrote that, and I know that is true, because God would have never meant it that way." But, can it be true instead that it's because of our selfish misguided "I don't see what's wrong with anything that feels so good," life style that on the whole, at least in this nation, we have abandoned the ideal that God is right and I am not? So much, that, "You know, I don't even need to investigate that any more, because I just know…!" Have you ever heard this? "If that's the kind of God He is, I don't think I can believe in Him." I certainly have!

I know how much our world has changed, and how much those of us who still try to stick to accepted Biblical standards have ended up becoming the ones who are "out of bounds, out of touch, and just plain out" on so many issues. I see how many of those previously accepted Biblical standards are being twisted to allow a new interpretation for what some want the Scriptures to mean. There seems to be little sacred anymore. We all have been affected by the things we see around us. That is why it is so vital to capture an in-depth teaching on honesty and truth. Too long have we stepped aside and watched that legendary plumb bob swing way past the center line of godly, biblical truths...honestly. Our society's NEW morality is patterned so as to make it impossible to express any particular rights or wrongs. Where little is either good or bad, but only "whatever I think anything ought to be, or could be, should be." A morality that is intellectually based, and allows no room for correction or understanding is pretty much where we have landed. Because what I think and what you think differ, the only thing left to debate, let's say, is, "Well I guess we're just different, that's all." So, without any perimeters, or let's say, without a set of rights or wrongs that the majority of people can agree on, what will naturally occur is anything one may want to be has to be accepted. Anything one wants to do, think, act out, like, allow, feel, accept or challenge is just fine. "You do your thing, man, and I'll do mine," mentality will divide us all. And a house divided, well it will fall, won't it? And here again, I am not referring only to our general population, but to our Christian communities as well. Hopefully not on as broad of a base, but still, it includes us Christians. And that analogy that I just showed you, simply put, is our current world view of things. Add to that a lacking of godly do's and don'ts, and our society is really headed for seriously stormy conditions, and in fact are already there. Now, once again I will defend my opponent's view when they say, "I have a right to think any way I want." YES, you do, and if that were all there was to this, I would not be writing this chapter for you to read. To those who faithfully demand their right to be unfaithful to God's standards for any reason, I am praying for you to know truth. My whole heart (and this is the reason I am writing this chapter to you) is bending with ultimate compassion for YOU, my Christian brother or sister who genuinely is a believer, but who has been infected with that world view of things. This really amplifies the truth of an old adage. You can't fit a square peg into a round hole, but with our current "don't tell me what to do," ideal, we, that is us Christians, are being systematically told to throw that square peg away, and to stop trying to make the hole square again. "I like it round the way we've redesigned it," is a common thought today. I know, ouch. Some will say that those old preferred moral standards haven't made any changes that didn't need to be changed. "I mean, we're just a little more tolerant than we used to be, right? And that's a good thing, isn't it?" You know, being tolerant is great, but not at the cost of shooting truth in the foot. Some even believe that what is going on in our world today is actually a good morality adjustment. "It's freedom, man. Don't you feel it? I can do whatever I want, and not feel guilty about it anymore." Nice, huh? Who wants to feel guilty? "It's you who should feel guilty for making me feel guilty with your moral self-righteousness." That may seem a little strong, even for today, but not as far out as many Christians would admit. Thus, the need to really investigate MY own personal, individual standards of what I am calling moral, and what I am considering immoral. That will help you set yourself up to discover where your honesty crosses with God's reality for truth in your life. It's way past time for all of us who proclaim to be a follower of Christ to dig, and I mean dig deep into a re-evaluation of my life in Christ. We can't and shouldn't want to change anyone's morality, so if you are not a Christian, relax. This chapter, like all the rest in this book, is not meant for you. On the other hand, if you consider yourself a Christian, meaning you have accepted God's free gift of life because of what Jesus did for you, then you seriously should consider what is moral and what is not moral, using God's handbook of instructions, not your own vain imaginations, as your guide. Or, I guess you could just put your Bible away and hide it from yourself so then, since you "don't know," you don't need to worry about all the things He may be leading you in differently than you now think. Here's an additional option. You can pick up a Bible and make it read just whatever you want it to mean for you. Of course, that is like telling God who He is supposed to be, instead of the other way around. You see, many Christians today are doing just that, and THAT, is the main reason for this chapter. Now, what is truly moral or not, from my stand point, isn't the point I am trying to make here anyway. But your morality is a great measuring stick that will illuminate either how much you want to be a servant of the living God, or how much you want your God to serve you.

No one needs to tell me how hard core I am making this sound. But sometimes we, and you better believe that I am including myself, need to hear it right up our noses so that we can finally come to grips with what Jesus said many times, "Let him who has ears to hear, let him hear!"

The real issue here in this chapter, anyway, is to put your honesty and your derived truths to the test. It's not about morality. So, I have decided that rather than me making a list of moral absolutes the way I see them, or to categorize what I see as God's dos and don'ts, I'll leave that up to you. My advice is strict though. Don't just go back to your own understandings of what is right or wrong. Read Proverbs 3:5-6 first, noting that there are three distinctive things God is asking of you BEFORE He will direct your path. But after you do that, seek what is right or wrong in your life from God's perspective, and don't be shy about admitting where you have been wrong all along. Praise Him if you have not been wrong all along, but make absolutely sure about your standards, that they match with what God's Word has for instruction. And above all, don't forget to pray. He is always available, and always waiting to hear you say, *"Help me Lord to see YOU, above all, and in all things."*

287

Difficult questions? Hard answers, easy answers, no answers, who cares?

There are some hard questions all of us have been called on to answer from time to time. And sometimes we deliberately avoided answering hard questions because, well, they are so difficult to answer. Maybe our answer would stir up such controversy that we would rather step around it, responding with something like, "Oh, would you look at the time, you know I just have to be somewhere right now." And then simply dismiss the question and walk away. Or maybe our response to one of those hard questions would leave us embarrassed to the hilt if we answered honestly, and we don't think that we could take that kind of rejection. Or, if we just couldn't avoid answering, feel that we would have to walk very softly on that particular issue because this one person we know most likely would get offended, and "I don't want to do that." And the worst response may be that we are tempted to lie, so as to avoid detection. Actually, another reality is that many Christians today "can't" come up with a good answer to some of the Biblical questions they may be asked, so they just avoid the situations where they think they may be asked. Let's explore some basic truths on this topic of answering difficult questions, so that you don't feel condemned when I ask you one of those hard questions. First, don't you know that this problem of having difficulty answering hard questions is the same with every one of us? Yeah, you're not alone. Secondly, do you not believe that the things that you might be embarrassed about are usually the same things most of us can get embarrassed about? So again, you are not alone. Thirdly, you need to know that since we are all human, and we all, referring to us Christians, face that fight or flight syndrome to either hide or lie when faced with one of those seemingly impossible situations? Yeah, and again, I say, you're not alone. Part of the reason that we continue to stumble is because we feel like our answer would not be understood, or it may be rejected, or would place us in some permanent, unpopular ugly box of some kind. And, finally, do you not know that in any case, it is our enemy who wants you to clam up, to hide, or to lie? Did you know that even if you do answer, and it is a totally correct rigorous instruction about one of God's precepts, it is still our enemy who wants you to fail, so that not only you look bad, but so does God? Additionally, sometimes a question that would be very difficult for one of us to answer, won't be for another. What it comes down to is this. When I, or you, feel threatened, or don't really have a good answer, for whatever reason, we freeze to some degree or another. Yes, all of us have or will experience that sometimes. With that being said, what I am going to do is ask you to answer a couple of very pointed questions to help you investigate not only what you believe, but more importantly, why you believe what it is that you do believe. Furthermore, I am only referring to hard questions you may be asked to answer about your faith in Christ Jesus and the Word of God. Finally, in the front end here, it's only going to be the two of you who hears your answer. That being you, and the Lord.

Let me begin with this. If you were asked, "Are you honest?" you most likely would answer, almost instantly knowing that any hesitation would give you away, "Yes, of course I am." You might even expound on that with, "What do you think, that I am not?" Truth be known, all of us would have to admit that there are times, but silently you likely would think, "I'm not deliberately dishonest, and I don't think I'm any worse than anyone else." Let me assure you, you aren't any worse than any of the rest of us. Be careful, though, not to think that you are better than any of the rest of us, either. Being honest is what I think; you know for the most part, I am. "I mean I don't go out of my way and try to tell a lie." And don't we all know that one special person we admire, and want to emulate? We may as well place a stamp on their forehead that reads "I am one of the only ones on earth who really is honest, *all* the time!" Like my mother, or your pastor, or your teenage daughter, well you know what I mean. We are sure beyond all doubt that one person wouldn't tell a lie even onto death. Although you may be right about them overall, they are none the less like all the rest of us, just human. Keep in mind that I am not saying that they, or you deliberately lie. But take a look at this. On the flip side of that "honesty" coin lies the word "truth." Truth is another word that can haunt, and should haunt us, because the truth in us is much more abused than the honesty in us, honestly. The words honest and truth have identical ideals, but do not have all interchangeable meanings. What makes it worse is that many of the untruths in us are by far less acknowledged than our dishonesty in us when either of them pops its head above the horizon of our consciousness. Truthfully speaking, the honesty in our bones will be much more truthful than the truth in us will be honest. "That makes no sense at all?" you question. It can be rather confusing, but therein lies the truth. Get it, "lies" the truth? I can also perceive you saying in negation, "Honesty and truth are the same, aren't they?" And I am so glad you asked, because here's another look at that. The entire human race, and yes that means you also, aren't nearly as truthful as we are honest. I know, and here is where those two words are often interchangeable. Truth, however, is almost always up for interpretation by someone, somewhere, where your honesty cannot be interpreted by anyone except you. You are either honest or you are not, and no one can honestly read your belly button to know.

Now, just because truths are up for interpretation doesn't make *your* truths incorrect. Likewise, it doesn't make *your* truths correct either. I am not suggesting that all the truths that you stand on need any correction. Most of them most likely don't. But it does mean that you need to very careful not to buy into just any truth, and I am referring to spiritual and biblical truths, without really putting it to a test, let's say against God's Word. And even then, with the help of many others who have made it their goal to do the same. Oh, and be careful not to depend on your life long best friends to confirm or deny any truth you are so sure of is correct or incorrect. They most likely became your life long best friends because they think like you think, believe like you believe, attend the same super market auxiliary shopping network, etc. So, if one of their hardened long-term truths that they are willing to die for is wrong, even if they honestly believe it, you likely will also. I know you will say, "Wait a minute, they wouldn't lie to me." I am sure they wouldn't, but if they are incorrect in some truths that they firmly believe in, you very likely will be also. You see their honesty and your honesty is not in question in this example. They, or you, genuinely believe, thus are being totally honest in your belief, but could be totally wrong about the truth behind that honest belief you are standing so full of resolve on. Okay, I can read between my own lines of type, here, the wonderings from some reading this and hearing just one single word, "WHAT?" Okay, keep reading.

Being honest is the easy part. Honesty is defined, mostly, as a deliberate attempt to not deceive. Or the reverse, dishonesty is the deliberate, knowledgeable decision to deceive. You are only a liar when you KNOW you are projecting what you know to be an untruth. So again, your honesty may not be at stake here, but that truth you were just honestly proclaiming might be up for discussion. Your interpretation of the truth, as you honestly believe it to be, may have come from a variety of sources that end up not being true, or at a minimum not all true. So, you're honest to a fault, and believe fully in the truth you are projecting, but it may not really be truthful at all. If nothing else you can be very wrong about what it is that you believe in, and that is my point. Following up with that is this. Given the circumstances, then, you may honestly be deceiving someone. Now, before I go on, I know that what I am pushing here about your honesty and your truths won't apply to everyone of us Christians, but it's probably good advice for you to investigate yourself in this with an open heart, just in case it does apply to you. And again, I remind you that I am referring to Biblical truths and standards. So, the next hard question I will ask is where do you gather your truths from? Here's a short list of some of the foundations that helped to form the beliefs most of us Christians hold as truth. In essence, where have we gathered our "to live or die for," truths from?

Did we acquire them from memories, experiences, both good or bad, our imaginations, or beliefs that we take away from each one of them? From the way we were raised? How my grandmother, mother, father taught, treated, or loved me, or just ignored me? How we were treated by the older brother or sister etc.? From school, my teachers, classmates, whether I was a good student, average student or bad student? Whether I was accepted by the "in" crowd, or rejected? Was I considered a nerd, or was I popular? Was I part of a very poor family, or did I come from a rich background? Was it our neighborhood, our family influence, and here's a really big one: what my own interpretations of real events were? Was it from my own personality? Am I an extravert, an introvert, or was I strong-willed which might well determine how I may interpret fairness in any given circumstance? Was I bullied, or was a bully? How about my failures or successes? What of my landlord's ideals, or a manager I used to work for that I looked up to, or totally despised? Was there a failed marriage? Did you come from a blended family? Our core beliefs are basically formed by all or any combination of all of our environments we have ever lived in. And there's more. Add to that list church, the Bible, Sunday school, Christian counselling, and all that goes with that. So, it doesn't take a Ph.D. for me to clearly see that many of those "I just know God would agree with me on this truth," issue has received its concrete footing into our lives from one or more of those foundations. Now, to be honest, that, in and of itself isn't so out of bounds, or unnatural at all. That is how we gain our maturity, and our wisdom. But the thing that is at stake, again, is about issues that pertain to our Christian lives comparing God's ways to my ways. To use a correct source, or Biblical foundation to make that comparison instead of any of those other foundations *only*, especially if I use my own vain imagination to "figure it all out," basically depending on "you know it just makes sense, doesn't it?" If your to-live-or-die-for truths are mostly, or idealistically, based on, "God loves everyone you know, so I think He understands where I'm coming from," you most likely will end up being deceived at least in some portions of your belief system. Your honesty, again, is not an issue here, is it, because I know that you are not lying about anything involving your beliefs. You are telling the truth as you believe it to be. But if those things that you hold to be "the truth," are mostly based on who, how, why, what, and when I was born, or the life I have lived, or been forced to live, and not on sound Biblical, proven to be correct standards, you may not even know what the truth really is on so many fronts.

So..., let me give you a little slack here. Many of your to-die-for truths let's say didn't actually come from your study of the Bible, but may be right on the nickel anyway. You may have had a wonderful set of life mentors, not necessarily biblical mentors, who really did give you a sound platform that ended up being biblical standards to grow and to stand on. Therefore some, maybe even most of your truths are genuinely correct. But until you honestly choose to examine all of them through the lens of God's Holy Word, you will not have been diligent in your investigation to know for sure. As long as you choose to believe something is truth, stubbornly standing on it simply because "I know God has to agree with that...," or, "I can't believe God sees anything wrong with that...," you may be missing the mark by a mile.

Ask those hard questions of that person looking back at you from the other side of the looking glass, and don't be too quick to discard the questions. There is a high probability that you have, again being normal, trained yourself to quickly come up with an automatic response "no there isn't," because if the answer would be "yes there is," they wouldn't be as much of a "to-die-for ideal," would they? Then whenever you think you have some really solid answers, sit down and relax, giving God time to speak back into your spirit. Some of you may catch the ball I am tossing to you and run with it. I'll pray that you do. I know that this exercise will reveal some things to some of you, that most likely you have already known about for years. What I am asking you to do is take a really long look at your personal Christian issues clear across the entire spectrum. Check out all that you honestly believe, and why you believe what you believe. Does it replicate the godly stance given to us from the Word of God? Or is your stance on any issue more representative of what your denomination teaches, or what your "oh so wise" sister has always believed? Or maybe you have for years simply purchased a "ticket to ride" on your church's, your pastor's, or friend's description of what God is like? Maybe you have just not been active enough to truly investigate for yourself what the Word of God actually says. Instead, having used that one commonly known tool that we all have…your own made-up interpretation of what you think, or hope God is supposed to be like. In addition, don't be too quick to condemn any political stance, or gender posturing, or anything else. Get to the root of God's truth in your honesty first. Deal with all those other issues later when you are on solid ground with God's Holy Spirit and God's Word. If you are a true believer that Jesus, the Christ of God, honestly truthfully was sent from God to deliberately die on the cross for the sole purpose of paying the debt that you owed, then trust Him, and get on board the only train to glory, and become His true disciple.

What is Mumbo-Jumbo, anyway?

OK, enough of all this repetitive mumbo-jumbo. All that then, leads me to what should be only a couple of hard questions for you to answer. I call them hard because if you are truly honest, you'll have to think on this for a while. And since it is only you and God who will hear your answer, you don't need to hide, lie, or be embarrassed. Watch out for your enemy, though, and pray, asking God's help to put your heart in the right perspective to hear a correct answer from yourself. So, dive in and actually, literally, look into a mirror and ask yourself. "Do I have some 'to die for ideals' that I have been calling truths, honestly for years, but may not actually be true? Could some of those "truths" of mine, more accurately be named semi-truths?" **AND, most importantly** now, is this. Don't just stubbornly pound on your chest, stick your powerful "I'm a man, and no one can convince me otherwise," chin out and not follow through with this. Or, cross your arms over your chest, put on your "you can't move me," attitude, saying, "I am a woman who has been through hell, so you're not going to change my mind."

And I just prayed for both of you to lower your guard to God, allowing His Holy Spirit to heal your hurts, keeping your humble guard up against your enemy, certainly, and check this out.

But you, child of God

It has been years ago, now, that I prayed and asked God with my whole heart, "What do you really want from me?" You know, it's an interesting quest, asking God to tell you what He really wants from you. If you are sincere from your heart, and truly are honest, He is faithful. What do you think God told me? Well, in other words, you are reading it. I had to take stock in my own life, understand that what I had allowed myself to think, to imagine, to respond and even to believe was not based exclusively on HIS truth. All my friends named me as one of the most honest people they knew. But my honesty was not up for debate, not to my friends, anyway, but the truth within me was. So, I asked God to help me completely change, not only my outward actions, but my inward heart's attitude. You see, it's like this. With some of us, sometimes, our spiritual eyes have been glossed over like we have cataracts on our souls. We have learned to accept anything from almost anyone who will stand up and state with confidence, "this is what God wants us to do." It may be correct, or it may be incorrect, but either way, we don't follow-up with any personal study to make sure. Or we just look into some of those issues with just enough study to find Scriptures that will prove *my* point and stop there. And it just seems to be getting worse. Additionally, we are so busy finding fault with anything, or anyone else, that we aren't able to come down from holding court, being judge and jury against any or everything we don't like, or don't understand. We quickly judge things we think are ungodly, or the reverse, things we "think" are godly, without first investigating any real solid truth within. Human nature does have its drawbacks. We have become so infected with "you know, it just makes sense" that we throw God out of the driver's seat, and plow right into the world's ways of expression on anything. "Just look at what they did, do, or are. Don't they know better? Why, when I was coming up, I…" We excuse our own attitude with things like: "I just know I'm right" or "We have to do something" or "I'm sick and tired of the way things are going" or "What are we supposed to do, we are all going to hell in a hand basket" or "I'm not a coward, I don't mind getting in their faces, someone has to…"

BUT, it's time to just STOP! Let's learn from Paul who wrote to Timothy, "But You, oh man of God," to help him, in the same way God's Word is helping us today. So, I'll say, "But you, child of God," look past what our human eyes are seeing, and start to see spiritually what God wants you to see. Don't make anything up, but rather back anything up with your new godly view. A view God has been faithful to give to you from His Word. Give yourself time, and trust in Him. Take a break, sit down and relax. "Be still and know that I am God." Psalms 46:10. The best thing you have going for you here is to take the time to investigate your answers to these hard questions. Starting with, "Do I have some 'to die for' ideals that I have been calling truths, honestly for years, but are not actually true?"

It's simple, but it's not always easy

I have heard it said "it's simple, but it's not easy." It's like a very large jigsaw puzzle you may have to put together. Starting out it looks very complex, but after you begin you discover that it really is kind of a simple task. It just takes time and a genuine commitment to follow it through to the end. That is why it may not be so easy. Imagine, however, the thrill you will experience upon completion. I am already praying that you, who has long ago accepted the truth of God, Jesus, and the Holy Scriptures of God, grow past our apathetic ungodly world view of things to become one of God's true ambassadors. It is simple, it really is, but since it requires effort from each of us individually, it may not be as easy as we want it to be. We are all on a different part of the same road. Some of you may well be past what all this chapter is trying to teach, and are sailing along as close to being in the center of God's will as anyone can be.

If that in fact, is you, then take the time to pray for and help those who aren't.

Author's notes; I hope you had fun reading this chapter. At some points I tried to toss some humor in there for you, but I also know that there has to be some confusion created here. The study of Honesty vs. Truth is a tricky business. Any supposed or inferred truth is, and always has been, and always will be marked with a target on its chest that reads "I'm for grabs, you decide if I am truth or not." Understanding our human nature, that being that I can choose for myself what is truth, thank you, is the one truth that helps to deceive us all sometimes. If you will be truly honest with yourself, you will identify easily with what I just wrote. But remember that it isn't your honesty that is at stake. And not only you, but all of us, it's the things that we hold true that can be disputed. What I am attempting to do here, is to get you to start thinking about HOW and WHY you believe what you believe. About God, the Bible, and your projected stance on some of the very hard issues our society is facing, and to do your honest best to discover error in your hard-core beliefs and correct them. Or, through your honest searching, using the truths clearly seen in all of God's Word, prove you have been right about your beliefs all along. But in either case, to not continue to seek other people who believe like you believe who will tell you

what the Bible says, or what you want to hear. Get into that
mirror of yours and ask that person looking back at you the
really hard questions in your life. But before you do, just ask
for God's help to have the scales peeled back from your eyes
for you to see what God wants you to see about His ways for
your life.

Be encouraged.
Great things He has done, is still doing, and will do in you,
if you are willing.
Be faithful, be at peace, and trust in Him.
YOU CAN DO IT!

But You
And Beyond

19

Blessed?

There are two things

"I am blessed," the man announced to his wife. "I have
everything a man could want. I have a great job, a house that's
paid for, a very decent car to drive, a nice patio to relax on. I
have my health, and money to spend when I need to, or want
to. I even have a dog that is house broke. We can eat pretty
much what we want when we want to. We have great insurance,
and a lot of time off from work to go bowling or play golf when
I want to, and the money to afford it. I have a great retirement
package, there's money in the bank, and well, what more does
a man want?" he said looking out their back patio door at his
six-burner grill just smoking away. He stood there
contemplating his good fortune, with a beer in one hand and a
hamburger turner in the other. "No, life just doesn't get any

better than this, does it? "Oh," he said turning around to his wife, "and did I mention good health?"

"Yes, you did, actually twice," his wife said uncompassionately.

"You don't sound like you think we are. Is there something I failed to mention?" he added.

"Well," she started and then stopped and just looked at him. "Are you sure you didn't miss something yourself?" and she said that projecting a semi accusing attitude.

"I can see something is wrong. What is it?" and he said that with his own attitude.

"Well, I am surprised, but you forgot to mention that we never run out of toilet paper." She concluded standing like a sergeant with both her hands on her hips, and a grin from ear to ear showing off her sarcastic side.

"Whatever," he said, "you know what I mean, though, we are sitting pretty good, don't you think? We are blessed."

"Yes dear," she kind of sang it to him again uncompassionately, maintaining that slight edge of sarcasm.

"You know that it doesn't appear that you mean that. Don't you think we are blessed?"

"Yes, I certainly do," she put her hand down and changed her attitude, "but honestly, my oh so blessed husband, you didn't mention that you were blessed because of your wife, your kids, your faith in God, our church, or our ability to give to others who are not so blessed financially as we are. I'm even surprised that I heard the word 'we' in your 'I'm so blessed' analogy. Of course, I agree that we are blessed. Very blessed, but don't forget why we are so blessed."

"Wow, you really do know how to knock the wind out of my sails, don't you?" and Sam Summerfield sat down hard in one of their kitchen chairs. "Wow," he said again.

"Samuel," she always used his full first name when she wanted to accent something more strongly, otherwise, she always called him Sam. "Look," she said and then she paused, took a step toward him and sat down beside him. She put her hand on his shoulder. "There is this one important thing," she began again but paused a second time. She even shuddered a little as she gazed out past the patio doors, "Ah, actually there are two things I need to bring to your attention. First, you are a good man. You really are, and I know your heart is in the right place. I know that you are grateful for all God has blessed us with. And I know what you were trying to say, and I agree with you. I was only pointing out the importance to, well, maybe put the latter first, meaning acknowledging that we are blessed because of what God has done for you, instead of the other way around, that's all."

Sam took his gaze off of his marvelous oversized six-burner grill he was so blessed with, and momentarily hung his head. "You're right of course. And I'm sorry I didn't hit on that. Certainly, I know that there is nothing that I have done to deserve anything we have, including you and the kids. I am sorry that I came off that way. I'll watch my thoughts better in the future. Melanie," he said looking at her. "You and the kids, except for Christ of course, are my biggest blessing. Really and

I thank you for being who you are, and pointing that out to me. I think that I need to pay more attention to what God has done, and not what I have done." They sat there together for just few minutes soaking in this blessing that just passed between them. And then, "But," Sam said looking concerned, "you said that there were two things. What's the second?"

"Oh, ah yeah," and Melanie stood up to make some distance between them, "ah yeah," she said again looking out through the patio doors, "I think your burgers are burning."

Well, what do you think? Did Sam save his burgers? Did he adequately make up with Melanie? Did he laugh, or cry? Did he learn to thank God first for all his blessings? Well, you finish the story any way you like, but both of them were and are blessed for sure, but in many more ways than that old money tree could possibly provide, and so is each and every one of us.

Most of the time it is simply a matter of discovery, or maybe the best word to use is acceptance. There are dozens of stories I can come up with in my life where something looked like, or felt like a major blessing, but turned out to be more of a curse. And the real blessing that came was seen sometime later when I discovered how God had protected me from something I didn't even see at the time. How about when we ask God for something that we just knew beyond all reason has to be granted, because God loves us, and because it is something totally unselfish, and it gets denied. What do we do? We have a tendency, sometimes, to complain, or wonder, "Are you listening God?" What about this? What happens when that "something" you believe you ought to have been blessed with, God not only denies you to have it, but gives it to your worst enemy instead? "Oh, the pain..." But then, of course in time we see that if we had been "blessed" with it, it would have really been a pain. Thus, the real blessing for us was being told "No!" Finally, after we realize what God spared us from, we find ourselves, or should find ourselves, following through with a prayer for that worst enemy of mine, so that what they did receive would in fact be a genuine blessing. Blessings really do come from only one source. "Every good gift and every perfect gift is from above, and comes down from the Father of lights, with whom there is no variation or shadow of turning." Additionally, though, they are manifested in a myriad of different ways. So much so that we will never see all the blessings He bestows on us on a daily basis. That is why He tells us, "Peace I leave with you, My peace I give to you." Be at peace and be blessed.

Blessings come in all the colors of the rainbow

Many years ago, on one average middle of the week work day, my eyes were opened to one of the most heartwarming blessings I have experienced to date. I was almost forty then, and worked in a fairly large factory. It was a metal fabrication company, and we manipulated all types of metal for industry in a myriad of ways. It was a very hot 7 a.m. summer morning as my work shift started. We had been experiencing a drought for the previous five or six weeks, and not only was it hot, but very dry as well. I think that the temperature that morning, even at that early hour was around eighty-five, with the weather man's prediction of reaching right near a hundred by midafternoon. That was outside, but inside our factory, because of our machines, and because there was no air-conditioning in the factory, of course, it was at least ten degrees hotter at the beginning of our work day. Now, not to over use the word – HOT, but the truth was that I had not experienced that kind of heat, for that extended period of time ever before. Right across from my station, though, maybe fifty feet away, they hoisted the one truck size overhead door, and intended it to stay open the entire day in hopes to generate some air flow. It didn't work. The air outside was almost a perfect still. My job was to load and unload steel tubes with fittings attached into and out of an automatic welding machine, so on top of all the rest of this hot, dry, and no breeze morning, my job made it even more hot. I was not in the best of moods to say the least. However, as I began to face my obligation head on, I decided to pray, but I didn't pray for peace, nor did I pray for comfort. I didn't pray for God to help me through my day. I prayed a prayer of thanksgiving, because I was reminded of people who didn't have a job to go to at all. Just minutes after the buzzer rang for me to start work, I took a very brief moment and looked out through that open overhead door to see the sun burning down on the parched earth, and began to thank God for my existence. I began to chuckle, because as I finished that first initial prayer, I started to hum the tune to *"whistle while you work."* Funny because my instinct was to sing *"gasp out loud while you work."* But my serious side took over, and I just ploughed into my job with that attitude of gratitude and started to thank God for everything, for anything, while I worked. I thanked him for the drought, because I acknowledged that He is the giver and taker for His good purpose, even the weather. I thanked Him for everything my mind could come up with. And the surprising thing was that the more I was doing that, the less I had to try to think up something new to thank him for next. It sounded like I was reading it from a book that may have been titled "Things to Thank God For." It was Someone other than myself who was adding to my list as fast as I was opening my mouth. The things I was thanking Him for just rolled off my lips like they were memorized. In addition to that, I was sensing an overwhelming feeling of God's presence with me as I worked. I certainly was hot, but I didn't even think about that at all, I just worked and worshiped God for anything I could come up with. It was a nonstop experience for maybe twenty to thirty minutes solid, until the buzzer rang for our first break of the day. My eyes shot up to the clock near my work station because I honestly thought that someone messed up and hit the break buzzer early. No, it was 9:30. Two and a half hours I had been there worshiping, and thanking God, but it honestly felt like maybe thirty minutes at the most. This is not an embellished story in the least, and it was the first time in my Christian life that I experienced what I called walking with God. I reminisced back on that time many times since, and likened it to Adam and Eve as they walked with God in the garden. That was a whole lot of years ago, but I still remember that blessing. I discovered that day that blessings come in all the colors of the rainbow. I just wanted to share that with you.

Nice!

We are all blessed beyond words just to draw breath. We are also blessed to know that because of what God has done for us through Christ, we are allowed to spend eternity with Him. So, the closer I am to walking, here and now, with my Savior who died for me, the more I see the blessings He has for me. Things that before I was His disciple, I didn't know or see. One of the biggest blessings I will ever know is to teach someone whom God has sent my way to become His true disciple. But a bigger blessing still is seeing that disciple being led to help yet another someone become a disciple of Christ. Nice!

Look to the stars

I never wondered much about this even up to my mid-thirties when I attended some rock concerts. I didn't get to go to many because I couldn't afford it. That was the only reason, though. I would have spent as much money as it took to see some stars, and would have traveled long distances, if necessary, just to get a nosebleed seat if that was all I could get. I did, however, get to see some real legends live while still in their prime a couple of times. I remember being awe struck like everyone else in this mega thousand seat arena, without even standing room only available. I watched with my heart pounding to some men and women who were bigger than life itself come out on a stage with such a show, that it made me think, "These are like gods, how great thou art." Yeah, it's turned around isn't it? But there I was, and not alone. I was standing in the midst of untold thousands of screaming fans, listening to a roar that put goosebumps on my goosebumps, and screaming right alongside of them. When the concert was over, all we could do was sit and dream in silence. We couldn't hear each other for another few minutes, after this almost better than life itself experience. I had no idea who or what I was worshiping.

Worship to the King of kings

I went to church this year on Good Friday, to silently remember what Jesus did for me. How He was unfairly, unworthily, undeservedly but willingly from His own heart chose to hang there for hours before death took his pain away. How He was crushed, broken, humiliated, insulted, and brutally murdered without complaint...FOR ME. Blessing? Sure, it was. That's what saved my soul from eternal destruction. His disciples didn't understand then, but of course in time they did. We understand now, don't we? We are blessed beyond any real reasoning any of us could truly have, but...just before I left the church when the service was over, I couldn't help but notice that our church had over three times as many empty seats as we had attendees. Now I know that part of the reason for that was because of our current health conditions, but truth be told, even before this current situation, our normal attendance still filled only half the seats available. I stood momentarily, and remembered those rock concerts I had attended so many years before. I know from talking to many that in the concerts that are being sold nowadays, the same scenario still exists. The heart still wants to *look to the stars*? Don't think that I am trying to bash rock concerts. I am not. What I am trying to do is lead you to enjoy your concert, but give all your worship to the King of kings, for He alone is worthy.

So, what it all means is this: When all is said and done, and when all the leaves, figuratively speaking, have fallen from the limbs of this *me* tree God has made. When all the Springs, Summers, Falls and the Winters of my life have dropped its last snowflake, and I am ready to close my eyes for the very last time, what should really end up being important to me? Well, from reading this book, you know what my answer is, but had you not read this book first and that question is posed, what could my answer be? I might complain that I didn't get all I wanted. I didn't get to do all the things I really wanted to do. I could say I was cheated, because I know a lot of people who did more, or got more. Or, I may take an alternate path in my thinking and say that life was fairly good to me, that I did get to do a lot of the things I always wanted to do. Or, I might even think, "well it's about time. I've been waiting for this moment all my life, because…" and I'll let you finish that statement. But of course, my real answer WILL be. "I AM SO BLESSED." When I walk across that threshold, I'll get to see, and say, "My God, how great thou really art." I'll know joy, peace and love like I have never known this side of His kingdom. But additionally, I will say, "How blessed I was to have lived my life from that special moment when I decided to follow Jesus in every aspect of my life." My last words to whoever will be there with me when my time comes, hopefully will be, "I AM BLESSED EVEN UNTO DEATH." The question is: Will you be? And I would say to you now, why should you wait until then to see what is important to you now?

———————————————

———————————————

Author's notes; Certainly, I know that you know you are blessed. The really tricky part comes on the morning after a major fault crashes our night before. Our lives are always in a state of flux. Start to practice saying to yourself out loud every morning, no matter what has occurred yesterday... "I AM BLESSED," and then take some time naming your blessings.

———————————————

Be encouraged.
Great things He has done, is still doing, and will do in you,
if you are willing.
Be faithful, be at peace, and trust in Him.
YOU CAN DO IT!

———————————————

But You
And Beyond
20

No More

I am just a man, NO more. I am also sinner, NO less.

I've walked down roads that were clearly marked "Don't Go!" But I went. I've lived my life from my earliest memory with the word "SELF!" imbedded on my brow. My sins against God, myself, my family and everyone else were so evident that I needed more faith to believe why God "would" forgive me, than it would take to believe whether or not there even was a God who "could" forgive me. The path that I chose to camp out on every day of my life until I was almost forty years old was the kind of life that all who heard even a part of it, would click their tongues, wag their heads, give up and quickly walk away from me in total disgust. I felt worthless, and I was self-absorbed, lazy, arrogant, and loaded down with not only sins against God, but sins against this world in just about every imaginable way one may think. Yes, even some illegal acts.

BUT...

Although I was still just a man, NO more, and I was still a sinner, NO less, I came face to face with the One who walked on water. I knew about Him all my life, but chose to simply put Him off until...until, well, well, one day when I prayed and asked Him to take over my life. And guess what? He did. I believed that with God's help I could walk off of any road marked "Don't Go!" and instantly start walking down many roads that were clearly available for me and were labeled "Please Go." The word "self" that I had allowed to be stamped on my forehead instantly vanished, and a new word took its place. The new word was "JESUS."

My sins against God, myself, my family and everyone else were still evident, but I was forgiven for every one of them. I was also given a new understanding that although I may have to live out some of the consequences for my actions, the day would come when I would walk out of that, and be known as a totally different person. The new path that I chose to camp out on every day of my life from then on was the kind of life that all who heard even a part of it, would first of all wonder if it was real or not. Secondly, they would either believe it to be true and want to follow its pattern, or if they walked away, were not giving up on me, but were giving up on God for the time being. My prayer for them is that they could see that the path they are traveling on is so unattractive that they would seek, like I did, the only One who ever walked on water.

GLORY BE TO GOD

At the writing of this book, I confess that I still am only a man, no more, and I am still a sinner, no less. If there is anything good that comes from me now, it's "Glory be to God." I took the step of faith to trust that Jesus is exactly who the Bible says He is. Then after some study and prayer, I took the second step of faith that left me choosing a path for my life that brought glory and honor to God. That step was for me to start to live my life, every day, in any way I could think of so as to be in the center of His teachings, and of course allowing the Bible to be my guide for that. That changed my life.

Author's notes; For the last time in this volume anyway, I will simply, quietly say...BUT YOU.

What comes to the Beyond for you?
Only you can determine that.
May God bless you on your journey in Him.

Be encouraged.
Great things He has done, is still doing, and will do in you,
if you are willing.
Be faithful, be at peace, and trust in Him.
YOU CAN DO IT!
